Resilient Voi

The aftermath of World War II sent thousands of Estonian refugees into Europe. The years of Estonian independence (1917–1940) had given them a taste of freedom and so relocation to displaced person (DP) camps in post-war Germany was extremely painful. One way in which Estonians dealt with the chaos and trauma of WWII and its aftermath was through choral singing. Just as song festivals helped establish national identity in 1869, song festivals promoted cultural cohesiveness for Estonians in WWII DP camps. A key turning point in hope for the Estonian DPs was the 1947 Augsburg Song Festival, which is the center point of this book. As Estonian DPs dispersed to Australia, Canada, Europe, and the United States these choirs and song festivals gave Estonians the resilience to retain their identity and to thrive in their new homes. This history of Estonian WWII DP camp choirs and song festivals is gathered from the stories of many courageous individuals and filled with the tenacious spirit of the Estonian singing culture. This work contributes to an understanding of immigration, identity, and resilience and is particularly important within the field of music regarding music and healing, music and identity, historical musicology, ethnomusicology, and music and politics.

Ramona Holmes is Professor Emerita at Seattle Pacific University where she taught ethnomusicology and music education for twenty-five years. She plays violin, sings, and dances as part of the Seattle and Portland Estonian communities.

Resilient Voices

Estonian Choirs and Song Festivals in World War II Displaced Person Camps

Ramona Holmes

LONDON AND NEW YORK

First published 2021
by Routledge
2 Park Square, Milton Park, Abingdon, Oxon OX14 4RN

and by Routledge
605 Third Avenue, New York, NY 10158

Routledge is an imprint of the Taylor & Francis Group, an informa business

British Library Cataloguing-in-Publication Data
A catalogue record for this book is available from the British Library

Library of Congress Cataloging-in-Publication Data
A catalog record has been requested for this book

ISBN: 9781032016054 (hbk)
ISBN: 9781032016108 (pbk)
ISBN: 9781003179290 (ebk)

Typeset in Times New Roman
by codeMantra

For my father, Charles C. Holmes, and our resilient Estonian family and friends. Thanks for the music.

Contents

Figures

Preface

What a treasure hunt this project has been! Studying the music of my Estonian family heritage began only as a side note to my music education studies. When I started graduate work at the University of Washington in 1974, I decided to connect the local Estonian music community. Having not grown up near other Estonians, I was interested in finding out about the music and dance of my grandparents. It proved a much richer experience than I could ever have imagined. I am forever grateful to Hilve Shuey, a Seattle-based Estonian dance teacher, who pointed me down this path. She took me into her dance group, encouraged me to work with the instrumental and choral music, and helped me understand what it means to be an Estonian American.

Many members of the Seattle Estonian community have been supportive. The University of Washington nuclear physics faculty included Dr. Juri Eenmaa, who was also an Estonian violinist and avid musicologist. He had a vast collection of music and many musical Estonian friends who helped me find sources in Soviet-controlled Estonia. He also introduced me to an Estonian singer, Ellen Parve Valdsaar, in Delaware who helped with early research. My early work included research in Estonia (at that time under Soviet control) about the old folk songs, which became the core of my master's thesis on Estonian *regilaul*. Dr. Hiromi Lorraine Sakata supervised this research and was extremely resourceful in guiding me through the ethnomusicological process. The Baltic Studies Program was founded in 1994 at University of Washington. This program brought Professor Guntis Šmidchens along with many new resources to Seattle for research in Estonian, Latvian, and Lithuanian culture.

Seattle also had an Estonian choir directed by Mrs. Aino Mägi, who fondly shared her stories from her years as a singer and choral conductor. Aino gave me many old scores and materials. Her daughter,

Taimi Ene Moks, helped translate the documents and added details to the stories. Aino invited me to interview her, and that began my Estonian choir festival research in 1991. She provided information and documentation about the song festivals from both East and West Coast Estonian American communities. Many choir scores she gave me had handwritten notations, originally used in the displaced persons (DP) camps; these piqued my interest in the WWII song festivals in the camps.

At West Coast Estonian festivals, I had opportunities to talk with other Estonians who had been involved in numerous historic choral festivals. Among those I interviewed was Inno Salasoo from Roseville, Australia. After that interview, Inno mailed me some wonderful artifacts, including carefully preserved choral sheet music used in the post-World War II choirs. This gave me a closer view of the choirs and song festivals that were part of the Estonian DP camps.

In 2008, I took a sabbatical from my work at Seattle Pacific University, during which time I traveled to Australia. The Estonians in Sydney have extensive archives where I was able to study issues regarding the Estonian choirs and song festivals. Estonian Australian archivist Maie Barrow was particularly helpful in pointing out the documents these archives hold, including many old WWII DP camp newspapers, photo albums, journals, and programs. While in Australia, I was able to interview Viktor Valk and Edgar Siimpoeg, members of the post-WWII transit camp Estonian men's choir that immigrated to Sydney.

Elga Mikelson is a Seattle Estonian who has frequently discussed choral traditions with me. Elga was a high school teacher in the Estonian DP camps and a translator for the Augsburg Song Festival. When she showed me her photo collection of the 1947 Song Festival in Augsburg, I was very moved by the tremendous joy shown amid the hardship of post-war conditions. Thus, the DP choirs and song festivals became a new focus for my writing.

Many Estonians who fled to America after WWII brought their collections of songbooks, concert programs, photos, letters, DP camp newspapers, camp reports, and other artifacts to the United States and Canada when they immigrated. Many of these treasures were donated to the Lakewood Estonian House in Lakewood, New Jersey, and are housed in the Estonian Archives in the United States (EAUS), which was established in 1969. A large portion of the collection was moved in 2003 to the Immigration History Research Center (IHRC) at the University of Minnesota's Anderson Library.

The IHRC housed an archive that focused on the study of immigration, ethnicity, and race. The archives are now a separate, though closely linked, organization known as the Immigration History Research Center Archives (IHRCA). It holds a large collection of documents pertaining to immigration and refugee experiences. They were able to link the large Estonian collection of materials with related holdings in Estonia, Sweden, Germany, and other countries. This is now the largest collection of cultural material on the Estonian diaspora. The IHRCA collection also serves as an ongoing research center. They offer grants-in-aid for researchers to come to study their collection. I received such an award for 2013–2014 and traveled to research there in March 2014.

The IHRCA collection is well organized and can be searched via the web. I was particularly interested in items from the WWII DP camps and asked to see the items in series 1:

Series 1 contains documents and papers regarding camps in US, French, and British zones of occupation—mainly about Estonian schools in DP camps, Estonian National Committees, National Groups and other organizations, Estonian Red Cross Committees, and UNRRA-IRO (United Nations Relief and Rehabilitation Administration-International Refugee Organization), as well as various documents (correspondence, articles, reports, memoranda, bulletins, newsletters, lists, meeting minutes, regulations, instructions, etc.) concerning DP-status and emigration. Series 1 consists of 7 subseries and 26 boxes (1. Camp Augsburg-Hochfeld, boxes D1–D6 2. Camp Geislingen, boxes D7–D8 3. Camps in US Occupation Zone, boxes D9–D16 4. Camps in French Occupation Zone, boxes D17–D18 5. Camps in British Occupation Zone, boxes D19–D25 6. Red Cross and Gold Fund, boxes D25–D26 7. Miscellaneous, box D26), where box D23 contains 2828 cards with biographical information on Estonian prisoners of war in the Uklei Camp.

This series did indeed comprise many important materials, including the documents from singers, directors, and composers from the DP camps that have been used as source materials in this book. The IHRCA staff helped me find other materials in the vast warehouse. The materials are stored in large boxes that need to be carefully pulled from shelves and placed in a secure room for research. I had emailed the list of boxes that I thought would be useful and proceeded to go carefully through artifacts from the post-WWII lives of thousands of Estonians.

There were many boxes located by the name of the contributor, so the names of choir directors from the song festivals (such as Virkhaus) were clearly important. Some records were sorted by the name of the camp, so information specifically about Augsburg and Geislingen DP camps was pulled. The collection also has the original note cards that were used by the UNRRA (United Nations Refuge Relocation Association) to organize more than 28,000 refugees. The cards are now held in large boxes, organized alphabetically by last name. This offered me a chance to find more accurate information about birthdates, spouses, children, dates of entry to the camp, and either dates of death or dates of immigration from the camp for the important directors and composers.

The city in Germany where many Estonians were housed after WWII is Geislingen an der Steige. I traveled there in August 2014 to visit the places where the song festival was planned, as well as to Augsburg where the 1947 song festival occurred. Many of the streets and buildings look just the same as they did in the photos from the 1947 song festival.

The materials used in this book come from a wide Estonian diaspora that encompasses Europe, Australia, and North America. All these sources combine to tell a story of an important time in Estonian history. This is the story of the Estonian choirs and song festivals in World War II displaced person camps in post-war Germany. My heartfelt thanks to my family, the many Estonian friends, and friends of Estonia who have helped me with this project.

Acknowledgements

There are many wonderful people who have helped me over the past forty years of this project and who have contributed to the story in this book. Many of them have gone on to sing together beyond this world. Early help in Estonia came thanks to my dear friends Urve Lippus and Malle Kiviväli and their families. Special thanks to Seattle Estonian community members, including Aino Mägi, Taimi Ene Moks, Elga Mikelson, Hilve Shuey, Juri Eenmaa, Elvi Urv, Linda Janson, Enid Vercamer, and many more. Many other Canadian and United States Estonians including Ellen Parve Valdsaar, Arved Plaks, Jaak Kukk, Taavo Virkhaus, Dr. Roman Toi, and Lehti Merilo have helped on the way. Thanks to Australian Estonians Raivo Kalamae, Inno Salasoo, Edgar Siimpoeg, and Viktor Valk. Maie Barrow was especially helpful at the Australian Archives. Thanks also to the IHRCA and the staff there. Thanks for the help finding photos to Elga Mikelson, Ants Toi, and Ilvi Turner. I am especially grateful to the fabulous Estonian American musician Liina Teose for checking my Estonian spelling and translations. Thanks to Arvo Vercamer, whose depth of understanding about Estonia, Germany, and cartography produced excellent maps of post-war Germany and Estonia.

My sisters, Juanita Holmes and Chris Anderson, and my sons, Justin and Brandon Hunter, have been tremendous dancers, singers, and travel companions as I researched this project. Thanks to my kind, patient, technology-savvy, wise, and loving husband, Ron Bekey, for helping me complete this book.

Abbreviations

DP:	Displaced Person
ECU:	Estonian Composers Union
EKK:	Eesti Kooride Keskus (Estonian Choral Center)
ESTO:	Estonian cultural festival (though all capital letters, this is not a true acronym, but a name used for the international festival)
ESU:	Estonian Singers Union
IHRCA:	Immigration History Research Center Archives, University of Minnesota
IRO:	International Refugee Organization
LEP:	Lääneranniku Eesti Päevad (West Coast Estonian Days)
SHAEF:	Supreme Headquarters of the Allied Forces
UNRRA:	United Nations Relief and Rehabilitation Administration

1 Estonian self-determination through music

The "Time of Awakening"

The story of the song festivals in displaced person (DP) camps begins with early Estonian vocal and choral music, the development of song festivals, and the musical path to self-determination. This tiny nation has a tradition of making singing a key element in its identity so as to provide resilience through times of extreme hardship. The tale of song festivals opens with the ancient *regilaul* folk song history and is enriched by later choral hymn singing. Together these are infused in many new choral compositions to make *laulupidu*, the song festival that is at the heart of Estonian self-determination.

Regilaul

Singing has a long history in Estonian culture. Communal singing was part of everyday life in the *regilaul* (folk song) tradition, which was first written down in 1632 (Menius, 1632, 1848). Regilaul include work songs for harvest and herding, ritual songs for weddings and holidays, and lyrical songs for pleasure. This was the primary vocal music in early Estonia. The work of a peasant culture allowed little time for instrumental music, though some bagpipe, violin, and zither music were used for dancing. One popular spring-time activity associated with regilaul—both centuries ago and in contemporary choral compositions—is swinging (Toi, 1980). Often regilaul aided the movement of work, including songs for cattle herding, housework, harvest activities, and fishing. Children's songs with specific movements were used to tell stories or to play games. When there is no specific work or game in the regilaul, singers sometimes use a walking step in a circle or a semicircle while singing. An *eeslaulik* (lead singer) usually leads the song.

These early folk songs were primarily sung in unison (Figure 1.1) with some two- and three-part harmony (Figure 1.2) (Holmes, 1982).

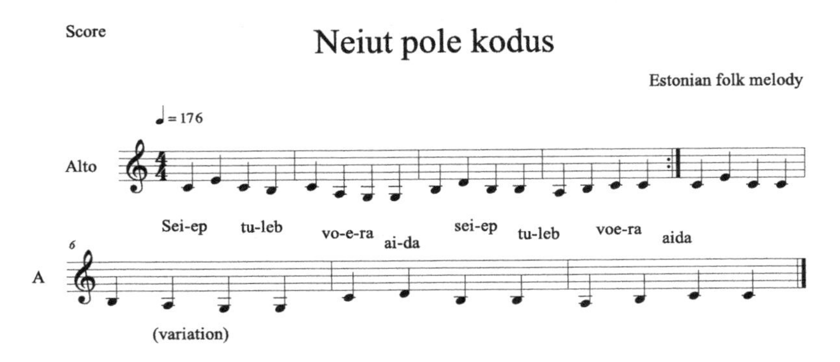

Figure 1.1 Neiut pole kodus (Women's Home) unison wedding song from Kuusalu, Estonia, Holmes transcription, 1982

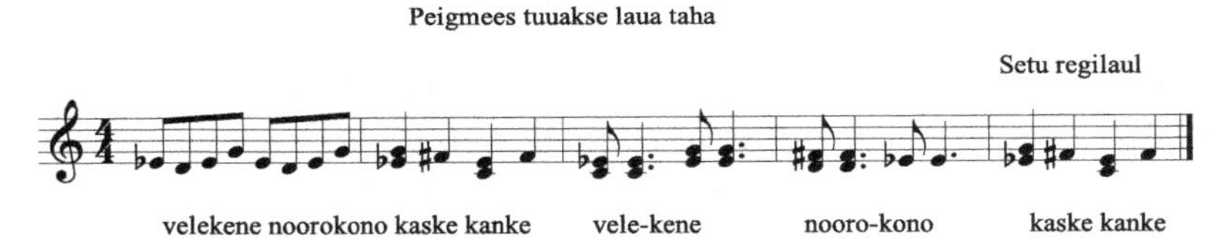

Figure 1.2 Peigmees tuuakse laua taha (bringing the groom to the table) two-part wedding song from Setu, Estonia, Holmes transcription, 1982

Regilaul melodies typically have a range of a minor third to a major sixth with a descending melodic line. The melodies are usually syllabic, with the text determining the meter. Estonian language puts the emphasis on the first syllable of each word, which determines the rhythm of the song.

The text for regilaul is an improvised poetic style known as *regivärss*. It uses alliteration and assonance, parallelism, and repetition with no set rhyme pattern. Some regilaul have a refrain that is typical for that context such as some wedding songs that have a refrain of *kaske, kaske* (birch, birch) or St. Catherine's Day songs that have a refrain of *Kadri, Kadri* (Cathy, Cathy).

The words are most often improvised by a song leader, who starts the first line solo and is joined by the chorus on the last two syllables of the line. The chorus and the leader then repeat that entire line. The chorus needs to guess the last two syllables in order to join in.

This is a practice known as *leegajus* (overlap) that works well in Estonian because it is an agglutinative language; hence, often the last two syllables are common word endings. For instance, the overlap in the following "Kiigelaul" (Swing Song) happens when a leader starts a line and then the group comes in on the last two syllables of the first line. Then they all repeat the first line:

Oh minu kulla kiigu**taja**
Leader **All**
Oh minu kulla kiigutaja
All

Still used in some settings today in Estonia, these regilaul form an important element of folk song music that is arranged, or used as an inspiration, for many choral compositions in song festivals. The use of regilaul today still brings out strong emotional ties to the homeland for Estonians everywhere.

Hymns and part singing through Protestant traditions

Some of the church choral music used in DP camps dates to early church compositions. Protestantism was initially brought to Estonia with Swedish rule in the sixteenth century. Eventually this included hymn singing as part of Lutheran traditions. A hymnbook published in 1638 included 144 songs in Estonian (Olt, 1980), but these early songs were not based on Estonian melodies, nor were they written to fit the Estonian language. Hymn tunes use regular duple and triple meters while regilaul's irregular meter is more determined by the Estonian text. Regilaul use tonal centers; however, they are far less tied to the harmonic progressions of major and minor that are important in hymns. The text in regilaul is somewhat improvised based on context, whereas hymn texts are set verses based on sacred topics. Many early Estonian hymns used melodies and harmonies written by Martin Luther or Johann Bach, while regilaul compositions are handed down traditionally without known composers. While regilaul was primarily single line or two-part, hymn singing introduced choral three- and four-part singing as an important aspect of Christian congregations in Estonia in the early 1700s.

This style of early hymn singing has become key to Estonian culture. It has also been noted that the "Protestant Reformation brought ideological foundations for a choir singer's identity" (Šmidchens, 2014:53). Many churches were built in villages where choirs sang on

Sundays, without being tied to the work contexts of regilaul. Moravian Brethren missionaries from Germany increased literacy and provided more printed Estonian material, including hymnals. These churches also worked to build a choral singing curriculum with musical literacy goals (Šmidchens, 1990). These church choral traditions have long been part of Estonian culture in Estonia and in the diaspora; song festivals also include sacred music in their repertoire.

Clergy were interested in both developing choirs and writing appropriate melodies for the Estonian language (Aavik, 1961:4). Gradually, choirs began to include secular repertoire and used more Estonian compositions. Collections of Estonian folk melodies had already begun with the work of German philosopher Johann Gottfried Herder, beginning in 1765. His collection of song lyrics in the two volumes of *Volkslieder* was an important first step in use of Estonian folk traditions. The first folk song collection adapted for choral use, *Vanemuise kandle hääled*, came in two installments (1868 and 1872) edited by Aleksander Kunileid and published by Jakobson. Choral compositions based on folk songs such as these would become an important part of the repertoire in DP camp choirs.

Estonian choral composers were beginning to emerge in the 1800s. Many of these composers wanted to study choral composition at the universities. The feudal system barred peasants from attending the renowned Estonian University of Tartu and so most of these Estonian composers studied at St. Petersburg Conservatory. Many important Estonian composers studied there before the 1905 Russian Revolution and built an Estonian choral style even while studying abroad (i.e., Härma, Kapp, Kreek, Lüdig, Tobias, Türnpuu, etc., see Chapter 5). In 1919 Estonia opened professional music to all at the Tallinn Conservatory and the University of Tartu. This began a long history of important choral composers, which went on to include such world-renowned contemporary composers as Veljo Tormis and Arvo Pärt.

Laulupidu: song festival beginnings

A sense of distinct Estonian musical identity was forming. The desire for self-determination was slowly rising. In 1869, long before World War II, the first Estonian *laulupidu* (song festival) was organized in Tartu with a brass band and 845 male singers. This first festival was organized by newspaper editor Johann Jannsen and the Vanemuine Selts (the Estonian theatre society named after the mythological character, Vanemuine) to commemorate the fiftieth anniversary of abolition of serfdom in Livonia (the ancient area comprising northern

Latvia and southern Estonia). There had been many concerts before this, but nothing on the scale of this newly organized song festival. Despite historic hardships, singing helped Estonians find the resilience and national unity that they desperately needed. As Olt explains,

> Today we can hardly imagine the difficulties of the organizers of the First Song Festival. The very idea of using the newly won liberty of movement, leaving one's home in the middle of summer, the busiest time of farming, must have been daunting. And the aftermath of the extreme crop failure of 1867 still made itself felt. Thousands had died of typhus and famine. Critics of the song festival proposed that its funds be used to bring relief to the suffering.
>
> (1980:21)

Russian administrators and feudal lords tried to delay the festival, hoping to stomp out the move toward independence. Jannsen and the Vanemuine Society were able to publish the songs before Russian permission was granted via Jannsen's newspaper. Through the newspaper, the organizers distributed scores and information to the choirs, so even when very late permission from the tsar was granted the singers were prepared. This festival was a clear success, and neighbors in Latvia and Finland soon began their own song festival traditions (in 1873 and 1884, respectively).

The Estonian song festivals began a new tradition of Estonian culture and became an eagerly anticipated national event. The rhythm of these periodic song festivals sets the tone for Estonian life and provides a national sense of strength and resilience. Jakob Hurt gave the opening speech about Estonian unity at the first festival saying, "Me ei või küll saada suureks arvult, kuid peame saama suureks vaimalt" (We cannot be great in number, but we can be great in spirit). The first festival is often referred to as the beginning of the "Time of Awakening" (*ärkamise aeg*) in the national movement for independence in Estonia. One anthem from the first song festival still often sung at festivals is "Mu Isamaa" (My Homeland) by Kunileid. Traditions from the first festival remained strong and continued in the World War II DP camps, as well as later in the Estonian diaspora.

Estonian song festivals have been held regularly about every five years since the first one. Festivals in Estonia have become known by their numerical order from the first festival in 1869 and were held 11 more times over the next 75 years. The frequency, which later became a five year cycle, depended on crops and wars. While there are many commonalities in how these festivals provide cultural continuity, the differences are subtle and important. The second song festival, held in Tartu in 1879, featured similar men's choral music and bands, with a stronger emphasis on Estonian national music. The Russian rulers were opposed to these festivals, so the next festival was timed to coincide with the birthday of Alexander II in 1880 so that permission would be granted. This third festival added mixed choirs to the concerts.

Under Russian rule, the tension between the government and Estonian festival organizers was a continual issue. In order to still have festivals during the reign of the tsar, festival organizers were forced to have song festivals designed to thank the tsar. Controversy over how much the repertoire could promote Estonian independence and how much it should be submissive was rampant. The choir numbers were mixed with "speeches by the clergy, who naturally enough preached concord and submission" (Olt, 1980:27). The festivals continued to be held in Tartu, adding more performance groups each time.

The fourth festival in 1891 was the first to combine the mixed choirs for mass choral pieces. Choral settings of traditional Estonian folk songs (regilaul) were added. This provided a layer of ancient Estonian culture to the soundscape. The fifth festival was held in 1894, with the tsar requiring a repertoire that featured Russian instead of Estonian music. In 1896 the sixth song festival was held in the new Tallinn festival grounds, where it has continued to be held since then. This festival added women's choirs. The seventh festival in 1910 added children's choirs and was the first to present all-Estonian compositions. World War I then drew the attention of the Estonians away from the festivals for 13 years. In 1923, the eighth festival was held in free Estonia using only an Estonian repertoire. Free Estonia continued to have festivals every five years, in 1928 (ninth festival), 1933 (tenth festival), and 1938 (eleventh festival).

During the freedom years (1917–1940), the festivals were much the same in that they featured national music and mass choral songs. Seattle Estonian choir director Aino Mägi, one of the interviewees for this book, was a young teacher and choir director at that time. She remembered singing joyously with her choirs on the Estonian coastal island of Saaremaa. Her choirs sang at the song festivals in Tallinn. The feeling at the song festivals was different: "We didn't have to say it so much then, of course we were Estonians. At first, they had to; then it was not so important, only that we love our country" (Mägi interview, 1991).

Following World War II, Estonia was forcibly annexed by the Soviet Union. While the song festivals continued in DP camps, they were also held in Soviet-controlled Estonia. The twelfth song festival was held in 1947 in Tallinn, Estonia, though the Communist Party used it for political purposes. The history of the song festivals under Soviet control and through the break from the Soviet Union is documented in the movie *The Singing Revolution* (Tusty, 2006). Information about upcoming song festivals in Estonia can be found at the song festival (*laulupidu*) website. Both in Estonia and in the diaspora, the laulupidu (song festival) is key to Estonian identity. Just as the Estonians in Estonia held ardently onto their song festivals, so did those in the DP camps.

The song festivals that grew out of the struggle for self-determination in the beginning of Estonia's history continued wherever Estonians needed their songs of resilience. While Estonians under Soviet rule held a festival, thousands of citizens exiled after World War II in DP camps kept Estonian choral music and song festival culture alive amid tremendous hardships. The song festivals from these DP camps are documented in handwritten scores, old photographs, and stories from conductors, singers, and audience members. This is the story of Estonian perseverance through choral singing and resilience through song festivals.

2 We will go home soon

Estonian displaced person camps in post-war Germany

The years of Estonian Independence (1917–1940), when song festivals were cemented as a national institution, were followed by foreign occupation under warring countries. As World War II began, Estonian men near the border of Russia were drafted into the Soviet army. Some escaped and joined the Finnish army. Life for all Estonians was disrupted as the Russian army swept through with a vengeance in 1940, halting the short-lived self-rule of Estonia. The Russians took over farms and deported suspected dissenters to Siberia or executed them. During this occupation, singing continued in private. Any public singing needed to be preapproved and pro-Soviet. Seattle Estonian Enid Vercamer remembered singing national songs in school during this era, but "with a few purposeful mis-pronounced words or carefully replaced words. The songs came out the same, phonically, but the words were either humorous or politically anti-Russian in tone" (Arvo Vercamer, 2014). Evald Alet remembered that the Soviet schools emphasized singing but "new and unfamiliar songs were taught, such as Big and Wide is the Land... etc., etc., which was pure Russian propaganda" (Alet, 1945).

Many important conductors and composers were vulnerable under Soviet scrutiny and often were arrested and sent to Siberia. One of choir director Adalbert Virkhaus' students tipped him off that his family was on the list to be deported to Siberia. He left Tartu in two hours that day in June 1941 with his wife and two children and fled to the larger city of Tallinn to hide. The Soviets came that night and, indeed, the family would have been deported if they had not fled (Virkhaus, Taavo, interview, 2008). Young choir director Aino Mägi was living on the Estonian island of Saaremaa when she heard that she might be deported. A well-known teacher and choir director, she was involved in political work like many professionals, and the Russians were suspicious of her. She explained,

> I took my two children, Taimi Ene, six years old, and Tiiu, four and half months old, and fled to mainland Estonia. In order not to attract attention, we wore summer sandals and took only a small suitcase with the baby's diapers when we left Saaremaa to Pärnu, where nobody knew us.
>
> (Mägi interview, 1995)

The Soviet occupation (1940–1941) was followed by German Nazi occupation (1941–1944). Many Estonian men were conscripted into the Nazi army—often after having just served and escaped from the Russian army. Many served in three or four different armies in the same year (Russian, German, Finnish, and/or Estonian). Some Estonians who had been conscripted into the Soviet army were captured and taken to German prison camps (Victor Orav's memoirs in the Australian archives carry many of these stories). With German troops moving into Estonia, many Estonians escaped, knowing they might be considered Russian sympathizers. Some escaped by boat to Sweden; others went into hiding as part of the "Metsavennad" (literally "Forest Brothers," the Estonian guerilla army).

When Soviet forces moved back into Estonia in 1944, the communists suspected that anyone who stayed in the country during the Nazi occupation must have been a German sympathizer. Deportation or execution were clear threats to any Estonian with land and who had been in the military, was a political leader, was a choir conductor, owned a radio, or just may have been reported as guilty of not supporting the Soviets. Throngs of Estonians escaped by boat, by horse, or on foot. Some escaped to Sweden through Finland or across the Baltic Sea (about 25,000). Others went to Germany across Latvia and Lithuania or by boat (estimated at 40,000–60,000) (Holburn, 1956:177; Saar, 2004:47–48). There were 1,133,917 Estonian residents in 1939 (Museum of Occupations, 1). During the war more than 81,000 died and just as many were arrested or deported. The country lost about 25 percent of the population. By the end of WWII, 100,000 Estonians had escaped and never returned (Pennar, 1975:27). Exact numbers are difficult to verify because so many died on the journey and identification documents were often altered to escape (Tammaru et al, 2010). The stories of those harrowing trips are chronicled in many publications (see Lie et al, 2007; Rebane, 2013; Maddison, 2015; Jurison, 2016).

As the Estonians were fleeing, they found themselves in the middle of serious battles between Russia and Germany. One particularly deadly incident during the Soviet Army's Tallinn Offensive was the bombing of the German hospital ship *Moero*. The attack killed more than 600 people on board, mostly Estonian refugees. The refugees who arrived in Germany before the war ended had to find housing and food in the war-ravaged country while also avoiding Gestapo who might think they were deserters or saboteurs. As Estonians traveled, they warily watched to see who was winning the war and who they could trust. Unemployment, along with severe lack of food and housing, made life in Germany difficult.

At first, these Estonians were still hoping to return to a free Estonia. In Gunzenhausen, Germany, Estonian refugee Alfons Rammo wrote to the commander of the US forces:

> I hope the present statement will induce you to regard the Estonian citizens as members of a friendly nation and as victims of Russian and German acts of violence, regardless of the fact that the USSR, the deadly foe of the Democratic Estonia, is at the present moment an ally of the other United Nations. I would call your attention to the fact that neither the German nor the Russian annexation of Estonia has been recognized by the Governance of the USA, England or France.
>
> (June 17, 1945 letter, IHRCA collection 2294–2358 MIC 112)

The 158 Estonians nervously waiting in Neresheim wrote to the US Commander,

> We Estonians here in Neresheim have come to West-Germany to wait here the arrival of either USA, English or French troops. We hope that after the break down of German military forces, the Peace Conference will again ensure Estonian independence and therewith the Estonian Republic, as it is said in the Atlanta Charta. It is our only wish to go back to our native land then.
>
> (IHRCA letter 25.4.45)

The Estonians waited and hoped that Estonia would become free, but their country was turned over to the Soviet Union by the Allies at the end of WWII.

Meanwhile, more than two million refugees were estimated to be wandering in Europe and experiencing similar traumas. This is described by European historian Tony Judt in his story of post-WWII Europe:

> Europe in the aftermath of the Second World War offered a prospect of utter misery and desolation. Photographs and

documentary films of the time show pitiful streams of helpless civilians trekking through a blasted landscape of broken cities and barren fields. Orphaned children wander forlornly past groups of worn out women picking over heaps of masonry. There was a sense of Europe being completely worn out and exhausted with varying levels of exploitation of Europeans by Europeans.

(Judt, 2005:21)

It is often said that surviving the war was one thing, surviving peace, another. The newly formed United Nations Relief and Rehabilitation Administration (UNRRA) and help from the occupying Allied armies kept large-scale epidemics and the uncontrolled spread of contagious diseases minimally under control, but complex post-war problems remained—minimal food, destroyed farms, rotting corpses, and the lack of basic healthcare.

Estonians arrived in Germany on carts through the forest or on boats across the Baltic Sea and found mass confusion as refugees sorted out where they could safely stay. Many who escaped to Germany were placed in refugee camps, also known as displaced person (DP) camps. There were originally 150 DP camps in Germany, though there were fewer later as the UNRRA consolidated the smaller ones for efficiency. In conjunction with UNRRA, the "Supreme Headquarters of the Allied Expeditionary Forces" (SHAEF) had 8,000,000 displaced persons to deal with in Europe (The Displaced... 1949). There were 32,220 Estonians in the DP camps of Germany by October 1, 1946. Refugees were roughly grouped by ethnic origin: Ukrainians with Ukrainians, Estonians with Estonians, and so forth. This allowed the groups to maintain their own culture and language, with no attempt made to integrate these groups into an already overpopulated and undernourished German community.

While these camps provided at last some chance for food and shelter, there was still considerable stress. This was a very trying time for the refugees, as noted by historian Mark R. Elliott:

Even voluntary migration can disorient ordinarily stable folk. But under the extreme duress of Hitler's forced movements, the surviving pawns of the Russo-German war had to cope not only with unfamiliar surroundings but with the memories of appalling living conditions and outrageous mistreatment and a whole catalog of attending psychological maladies. Helping keep refugees off balance were: the strain of unemployment and idle hours; feelings of isolation, helplessness, and depression; and anxiety about the future. (Would the Soviet Union move from Cold War to an

> invasion of Western Europe? Could they remain in an unfriendly Germany? Would they be forcibly repatriated? And would America or some other country take them in?)
>
> (Elliott, 1982:180)

Searching for family members who had been taken as prisoners added to the stress for many Estonians. Since they had been forced to join both the Russian and German armies, there were also Estonian prisoners of war in both Eastern and Western Germany. An estimated 6,000 Estonians had been imprisoned by the Allies and 5,500 by the Soviets. Most Estonian prisoners were later placed in DP camps after considerable pleas from family and friends were sent to SHAEF.

Toward the end of WWII, the Allies had sought the help of the Soviets during a meeting in Yalta. Many decisions the Allied leaders made in 1945 when establishing conditions for peace—this Yalta Agreement—directly affected Estonian refugees. Post-WWII Germany was divided by the Allies into four occupation zones, controlled by the United States, Great Britain, France, and the Soviet Union. The establishment of Soviet zones of influence, which included Estonia and much of Eastern Europe, effectively meant that the Estonians would be considered Soviet citizens by the Soviet government. The agreement to forcibly repatriate Soviet "citizens" after the war proved to be a serious problem for Estonians.

The Soviet government insisted that both prisoners of war and refugees who were from the areas they now controlled should be "repatriated." Most of these prisoners and refugees knew that they would be considered collaborators—returning to their homes meant imprisonment or death. Many were nonetheless forcibly repatriated. Refugees who had narrowly escaped capture by the Russians knew well that friends and family had been sent to the Soviet Gulags or had been killed. This policy was so frightening that "many committed suicide on the spot, using sharpened pieces of metal and utensils to cut their own and each other's throats and wrists" (Rebane, 2010). Taimi Ene Moks, even as a young child in the camps, remembers,

> You had left your home and fled to save your life, but now the Allies were about to send you back to the Communists. People who were returned to the Communists committed suicide or pleaded to be shot instead of being sent back in such numbers that finally the West noticed and forced repatriation was discontinued.
>
> (Moks, 2014:3)

Many desperate pleas were written by Estonian refugees and their supporters and sent to the UNRRA and the British, American, and French armies. The dangers of being sent back to countries subsumed into the Soviet Union were so terrifying that 530,000 Estonian, Latvian, and Lithuanian refugees became "non-returners" (Elliott, 1982:174).

Post-war Germany had very different repatriation policies in the Soviet, English, French, and American zones. While initially all refugees were expected to be repatriated, slowly information trickled out to the refugees that the English and American zones would let Baltic refugees stay in the DP camps without forced repatriation. Allied military forces were getting mixed messages at first about the actual impact of the Yalta Agreement as to expectations in the different zones. American zone camps began to review the directives about forced repatriation. The Baltic DP representatives from Estonia, Latvia, and Lithuania wrote a joint letter to General McNarney of the US Forces in Frankfort:

> We feel our duty to inform you that in connection with the announced intention of UNRRA to carry out a new, general and complete screening of DPs in the American Zone, the hearts and minds of the Baltic DPs, Estonians, Latvians and Lithuanians are in a state of intense agitation. We know that Soviet Russia has the greatest interest to get Baltic nationals in her hands and it seems that there are some tendencies for pursuing of a policy which at its end practically may lead to the extermination of the remnants of Baltic nations who have found a refuge in the occupation zones of the Western Allies.
>
> (1945 letter in IHRCA collection)

The American leaders told US zone commanders that they could

> quietly ignore the Soviet line that all people originating from areas within its new (1945) borders were Soviet citizens and thus subject to forcible transportation under the Yalta accords. Western governments refused forcibly to repatriate people who had not been Soviet citizens before the Second World War.
>
> (Shepard, 2010:84)

This was not an officially written response, but a clear understanding.

Although this point was left officially unresolved, Allied commanders, including British zone commanders, were instructed to apply their interpretation to the situation, not that of the Russians.

> 'For your own information and guidance, (but *not* that of the Russians)', British commanders were told in July 1945, 'Latvians, Estonians' Lithuanians and Poles whose homes are east of the 1939 demarcation of the Curzon Line will not be repatriated to the Soviet Union unless they affirmatively claim Soviet citizenship'.
>
> (Shepard, 1988:84)

It became imperative for Estonians in the Russian zone to find their way into the English and American zones.

As they moved into camps, Estonians needed to verify their DP status, which was based on place of birth, the date one fled their homeland, and the assurance that one was not a Nazi. The process of verifying credentials was tedious. Many Estonian refugees had fled quickly, often during battles or with no time to pack, and, therefore, carried few documents. One refugee remembered,

> Summer most of the time for the adults was taken up standing in long lines to be interrogated and have inspected whatever documents that had survived the war. It was confusing who actually ran what part of the interrogation and screening of the refugees.
>
> (Rebane, 2010)

Another recalled,

> To establish your status, there were screenings on top of screenings, and you better not misstate anything you had said previously. Many people had to adjust their working histories to make sure that nothing could be interpreted as their being Nazis. The anxiety level was tremendous.
>
> (Moks, 2014:3)

The loss of DP status was particularly worrying for women whose husbands had been forced to serve in the German army. Many Estonians were in prison camps because they had been forced to work for the Nazis or to be in the Nazi army. Estonians already in the DP camps began to advocate for their family members in prison camps. In a letter to the US Army, typed in very clear English, one Estonian mother implored, "Do not drive us to utter despair and do not add to our psychological sufferings. Please await the instructions from the officials to whom these memorandum are sent" (IHRCA letter, 1945). It was found that "it was in practice impossible to decide whether Baltic men who had served in the German army had done so voluntarily or under compulsion," so the policy quietly became "a double standard by which non-Germans in the Waffen SS were treated far more leniently than their German counterparts" (Shephard, 1988:216).

Considerable moving between camps helped Estonians get to their desired zones, where they were relatively sure they would not be sent to the Soviets. Eventually there were 31,221 Estonians in German DP camps, of whom 53 percent were in the American zone, 43 percent in the British, and 4 percent in the French. About 10,000 Estonians lived in Germany but outside of the camps (Estonia's Occupations Revisited, 2004:48). The International Refugee Organization (IRO) later helped 27,096 Estonians in DP and prison camps emigrate from Germany to Australia, Canada, Sweden, the USA, and England. A small number died or stayed in Germany or emigrated to other countries without the help of the IRO.

It has been noted that "a significant number" of Baltic refugees "were professionals, academics, intellectuals and artists, who were well versed in national culture and politics, who had a substantial stake in the native land and who perceived themselves as having been torn unwillingly from home soil" (Carpenter, 1996:1). These refugees had a strong interest in keeping their cultures alive, especially in the DP camps. The refugees "had abundant free time and little or no financial worries; and although Allied authorities proscribed political associations, they encouraged cultural activities and organizations" (Carpenter, 1996:1). The Estonians had suffered greatly and had much hardship ahead. They wanted to do more than survive—they wanted to maintain and celebrate their heritage. As Estonians established new lives built on their traditions in the DP camps of post-WWII Europe, a new era began. Their new lives would certainly include singing to uplift spirits and to preserve a culture forged by song in times of extreme adversity.

Rebuilding life in the displaced person camps

Herculean work was underway in Europe as the Allies tried to provide aid for the multitude of refugees. One strategy was to group people by ethnicity so that they could work together to build their own communities with familiar government, schools, and social ties while maintaining their native languages. Estonians were grouped at several DP camps in Alt Garge, Ansbach, Augsburg, Blomberg, Geislingen, Hanau, Ingolstadt, Kempton, Lingen, Lüübek, Memmingen, Oxford (near Dannenberg), Valga laagri, Wasseralfingen, Wielandshagen, and other small camps.

The largest concentration of Estonians was in Geislingen, Germany, where an entire village was established with Estonian stores, schools, and businesses. *Geislingen an der Steige* means "Geislingen on the climb," as it has steep hills going up from the river valley. It is just south of Stuttgart, so many residents from Geislingen went into the city to work and came home to the village on the weekend. The beautiful German village had been a retreat for Nazi officers and had come through the war almost unscathed.

As shown on many beautiful postcards, Geislingen an der Steige was a lovely resort. During the war, the Württembergische Metallwarenfabrik factory that produced famous stainless-steel flatware was commandeered to produce arms for the Nazis. After the war it was converted back and still produces world-class stainless-steel cutlery, flatware, and cookware (Figure 2.1).

During WWII, Geislingen housed a concentration camp with 2,300 prisoners brought by the Nazis from Yugoslavia, Russia, and Poland for forced labor. When the prisoners were freed and sent home, their meager barracks were vacated. In May 1945, Geislingen German residents in 170 local houses were given only 24 hours to vacate their lovely private homes. Each of these houses would be used as a home for

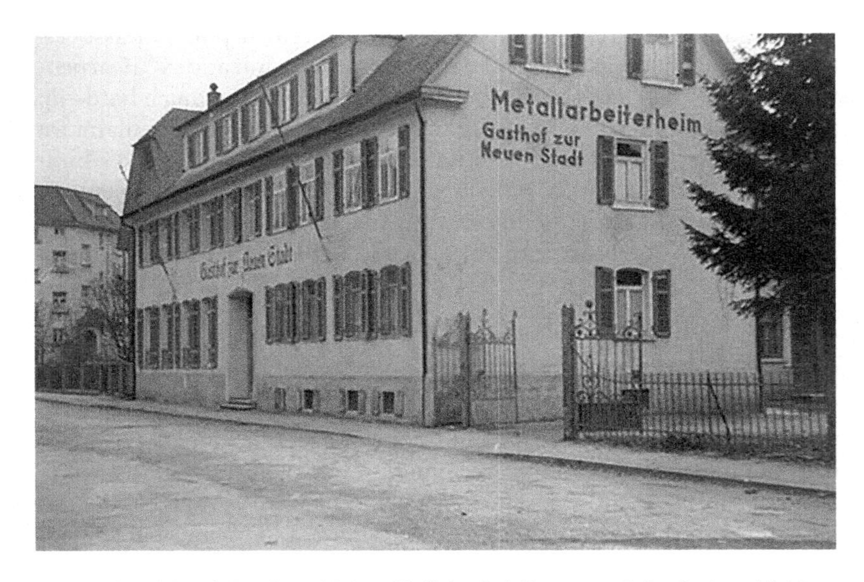

Figure 2.1 Metal Workers Union Hall in Geislingen and der Steige, 1945
Three-story Bavarian building with shutters on windows

eight Estonian families. The UNNRA prepared to house thousands of Estonian refugees in the former concentration camp barracks and private houses of this tiny village in a site known as UNRRA Camp 615.

Three thousand Estonians from many smaller camps were transported by the Allied forces and grouped in the barracks and private homes turned over from Germans for use by the UNRRA. Maps of the Estonian districts were made in the Estonian language. The camp opened October 11, 1945, with more Estonians arriving on their own. Very quickly, numbers swelled to about 4,000 and to as many as an estimated 4,500 by the end of the year.

Each community in the UNRRA had its own supervision and administration, with self-regulating boards. The Geislingen Estonians held democratic elections for a board of 15 members to set up the camp rules and principles. Within the first year, Estonian DPs had established churches, schools, saunas, choirs, theaters, a Red Cross, YMCA, YWCA, a dressmaker's workshop, a shoemaker's workshop, and more. Estonians attempted to grow some of their own produce and make some of their own drinks, even learning to make the long ice sticks used to produce just the right temperature for making local, Geislingen-style beer (Figure 2.2).

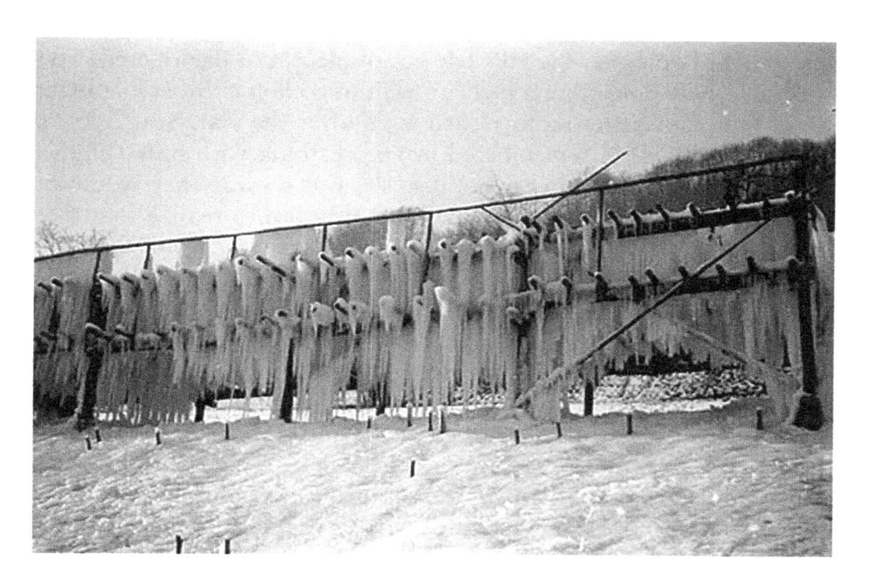

*Figure 2.2 Eisgalgen (*Icicles) used to make German-style lager, Geislingen 1945

Bridge with rows of 50 icicles and snow on the ground

Every Estonian in the DP camps had an escape story that involved hardship and loss. "Of 493 high school students in Geislingen who attended the school from 1945 to 1948," Helle Martin notes in her personal history saga,

> those who lost family members were distributed as 63 who had been deported to Siberia, 9 who had been killed, 12 who had been killed in the war, 11 who had been killed during a bombing, 116 who had been lost (not known where), and 161 who had stayed in Estonia. Of the 161 who had stayed in Estonia were 55 fathers, 51 mothers, 29 brothers and 26 sisters.
>
> (Martin, 2009:75)

To help those who needed support, be that in caregiving or economic, each camp had a Social Committee of the Estonian National Assembly Center. In Geislingen this included a place for elderly and invalid DPs, a "pupil's hostel" for children with no parents, three "sewing points" where mothers could sew for a small profit, and a clothing barter station (Estonian Displaced Persons' Assembly, June 1949).

The camps themselves were a welcome relief after war, but they were only designed to be a temporary solution. They provided food and shelter with some social services. They were never meant to be permanent homes, so the DPs felt out of place and disoriented. This was not a new home, but a place to wait to go home. Most Estonians had left home expecting to return soon after the war. Seattle Estonian Elga Mikelson remembered leaving Estonia with only summer clothes in her small suitcase because she was so sure they would be back home before winter. But as the DPs began to realize that they would probably not be able to safely return home, the joy of the war's end faded and turned to hopelessness amid lasting destruction. There was a general sense of futility, and many adults sat in their barracks and "endlessly talked, of the hopelessness of their situation" (Wyman, 1998:107). The UNRRA recognized that there was much rebuilding needed in DP communities. Attempts were made to encourage camp members to "set up their own churches and religious groups in an attempt to dampen down some of the worst excesses, and also to provide the demoralized men and women with some much-needed spiritual succor" (Lowe, 2012:107). With few resources available, the officials tried to help the refugees as they started to build schools, churches, and communities and began to rebuild their lives.

Not all DP camps were the same and the placement of ethnic groups in separate camps made that more obvious. There appeared a hierarchy of nationalities among the camps, through which administration was determined. According to UNRRA reports,

> [A] clear hierarchy emerged, with the Balts and the Jews at the top, and the Poles and 'mixed camps' at the bottom. The Baltic camps contained a high proportion of professional people, such as bank managers, engineers and civil servants, and had developed complete democratic institutions at an early date and in general had 'a complete constitution'.
>
> (Shephard, 1988:271)

This meant that the Estonians camps were essentially self-governed, with their own network for police, food supply, and administration; the UNRRA needed to do little to facilitate them. The UNRRA printed scrip for use only in the DP camps. Very basic food provisions, housing, and self-government were in place, but there were still great needs.

The camps were physically adequate but emotionally trying places to live. The psychological pressure of being in unfamiliar surroundings with unsure futures was formidable. Some refugees talked of depression and nervousness. Many noted that there was no sense of gaiety, they felt that it was almost out of place to be joyful and that they could only focus on painful memories. Other factors added to the pressure, such as worry about friends and family left behind and concerns that the Soviets would take over Germany. The lack of control over the future led to a sense of loss of self-respect. Estonians were used to being self-reliant and were uncomfortable having to accept so much charity. Many were farmers who missed having their own land to work. Others were musicians or artists who were used to performing regularly. Careers were put on hold as focus was put on paths to emigration. Professions were hidden as rumors of immigration requirements for only laborers surfaced. However, amid the problems, this holding period gathered cultures together in ways that helped heighten a sense of ethnic identity. Estonians, and many other groups in DP camps, had time together to solidify their cultural character in ways that helped them carry that identification with them out into the diaspora.

Building a new cultural life

Merely surviving the camps was not enough for the Estonians. They wanted to thrive. The UNRRA reported that Estonian refugees included many artists, actors, writers, and 175 professional musicians.

These culture advocates were eager to continue their work. As with their Baltic neighbors, the Latvians and Lithuanians, a short-lived freedom era (1917–1940) meant that the Estonians had a new nation to promote. One way they could do this was by immersing themselves in the camp system, building schools and choirs, administering the camps, and participating in any way possible. Estonians strove to have the most beautiful and healthy camps possible, with strong schools, efficient governments, and professional-level arts. They chose to have music at the center of their camps. Camp newsletters were established to disseminate information, including "Eesti Rada" in Augsburg, "Eesti Post" in Geislingen, and "Kauge Kodu" in Kempten.

Amid the chaos and confusion, it was imperative to Estonians that they build community and maintain their culture. The UNRRA was particularly supportive of these goals. Schools were established in each native language. A Baltic university was established near Hamburg and an Arts Institute near Freiburg. In September 1946, a directive came from the UNRRA to develop a short-term project to enable Baltic DPs to study together at the Museum of Hamburg History. The idea was to have a university with classes in English and German, which, they stated, was for students "whose academic careers and training have been interrupted by war profitably to fill a period of time prior to their return to their proper training or profession" (Järvesoo, 1991:78). This was designed only for Baltics in the British Zone and only for six-month periods. No fee was charged for this university.

Most of the Baltic University program was designed for science and mathematics. Botany professor Richard Kaho (1885–1964) also taught violin. Two professional musicians taught at the Baltic University: Latvian choral conductor H. Pavasara and renowned Estonian conductor Arkadius Krull. Some Estonian students there studied composition, with Estonian composers E. Öpik and Arkadius Krull. At the spring community celebration, the University Choir sang three Baltic songs, including a piece by Estonian composer Miina Härma.

Kindergarten, primary, and secondary schools in each camp started immediately. Describing her life as a young student in the camps, Martin notes, "There were many former teachers from different parts of Estonian and also some professors from Tartu University, the level of our education there was quite high, in spite of lack of books and teaching materials" (2009:70). In 1945, the Estonians DP camps included 19 kindergartens with 640 students; 33 primary schools with 1,160 students; and 11 secondary schools with 780 students. There were 58 teachers, 38 of whom received salaries from the IRO. Parents volunteered for the unpaid positions and did the cleaning of classrooms. Some textbooks were written and printed by the parents in the communities as paper and printers became more widely available. Some books were brought from Estonia. Seattle Estonian Aavo Kalviste left Estonia as a young teenager with one suitcase that held only his Estonian encyclopedia. That became one of the main reference books for the high school that he attended. Many well-educated Estonians were the teachers in these schools, including Elga Mikelson, the translator at the 1947 Augsburg song festival who also provided many of the photos in this book.

Geislingen was "like an Estonian town with all of its organizations" (Martin, 2009:72). Estonians remember the excitement during the early establishment of the Geislingen cultural community. George Rebane, who was a school student in Geislingen, wrote about the start of the community, saying,

> [O]ur camp quickly sprouted a newspaper, camp administrative office, and a post-office to send mail between the three DP camp neighborhoods in Geislingen. Soon we had a clinic, choirs (more than one of course), the obligatory Evangelical Lutheran church, theatre and a school system (K-12) for the 1,000 of us of school age.
>
> (2013:4)

The two primary Estonian religious denominations, Lutheran and Orthodox, both were provided space in the camps as needed. In Geislingen there were five Lutheran pastors and three Orthodox priests, who immediately got services started. These churches all included choral music as a key component of their worship.

Many professional actors, musicians, composers, and dancers had come to Geislingen. There were "about seventy different productions during these four years, which included the three operettas, many plays and many concerts" (Martin, 2009:79). The Estonians at Geislingen immediately formed the "Arts and Theater Section" and began to have performances. These performances included theater, dance, church, and, of course, choral concerts. The local theater building, Jahnhalle, (John's Hall) was designated for use for Estonian events. This large hall accommodated theater, music events, dance performances, puppet shows, opera, and more.

Life in the DP camps was not easy. Documents show that there were many ways in which DPs coped with their aimless lives as refugees. Some of them drank heavily, others found some sort of work.

For many Estonians, they threw themselves into the cultural activities of church, theatre, schools, and a wide range of community groups. At the center of each Estonian cultural activity were choirs that provided the hope, sense of Estonian identity, and resilience required to thrive amid the trials of refugee life.

3 "So we decided to start a choir"

Forming choirs in the DP camps

As the Estonians entered displaced person (DP) camps and began to build temporary communities, one of their main priorities was to preserve their cultural heritage. Camp choirs kept many Estonian singing traditions alive. Forming choirs was "a natural instinct to keep alive the mother tongue and mother country" (Toi, 7/29/2013 interview). As the camps grew, mixed choirs were formed, and more elaborate concerts were arranged. Sometimes the concerts included solo pieces as well as choir performances.

While the displaced persons needed to do such basic things as prepare food together, they began choirs at the same time. At the Alt Garge camp, the choir began in 1945, as Seattle Estonian choir director Aino Mägi narrates:

> Food was prepared in a common kitchen. Next to the kitchen was a big hall for dining. During the day we started using the hall for teaching children and organized a make-shift school. Soon people started using the hall for social gatherings. Our favorite pastime has always been singing. In the hall was a surprisingly good piano. The army officers heard us singing and liked it. They invited us to sing for their troops. So we decided to form a choir and I was asked to direct.
>
> (Mägi interview, 1991)

Aino Mägi built the choir with minimal resources, noting, "In the beginning I organized a group of young ladies to sing light songs. Everything was done by memory," as there was no sheet music available (Mägi interview, 1991). Not every camp had a piano available, so other instruments had to be used. Vaike Pruul, the daughter of choir director and song festival leader August Pruul, remembers, "Somehow he had managed to bring out his violin from Eesti and when piano and organ were not available [in Hanau DP camp], he would take out his violin and give tunes with that" (Pruul email, 2013).

The choir in Alt Garge was encouraged by the UNRRA and so they went in trucks (arranged by camp managers) to entertain soldiers. The singers were all young blonde girls, many dressed in folk costumes. Aino cheerfully recalled how alive she felt wearing an embroidered silk blouse and a folk costume skirt with red and white stripes; "my sister Salme took altos under her wing and a ladies' choir of 20 was under way. We lived in English Zone. We entertained English soldiers in their various camps. We were quite successful with our cheerful songs." They sang light songs without music, mostly two-part, soprano and alto such as "Lepa lind" (alder bird). She noted that "the Latvian choir sang more serious music, but we did not have men, so we could not do mixed choir" (Mägi interview, 1991). After singing they danced with the soldiers. They also went to other DP camps to entertain. Later, more refugees came to this camp. Suddenly there were some good male singers, including Mr. Ottan from the Tartu University Choir. The women's choir was discontinued and a mixed choir was started (Figure 3.1).

British soldiers in Alt Garge were helpful with organizing choirs. Mägi remembered that "adults needed something to do. There was no work to be had since Germans themselves had no work" (1996:51). The army and the UNRRA supported the development of choirs because they helped keep people happy and busy (Vesilind interview, 2014). The soldiers and relief workers were indeed impressed with the choirs and the general organization in Estonian DP camps. It was noted that their camps were

> clean, well-organized places run by the inmates' elected representatives, with every available inch of space put to good use, growing flowers and vegetable; the children properly taught, the women producing beautiful textiles, and, to cap it all, their choirs sang brilliantly.
>
> (Shepherd, 2010:157)

Clearly being part of these choirs helped boost morale immensely for the singers as well as for the audience. These groups performed for local audiences with great appreciation.

In the Alt Garge camp, the performances helped "relieve tedium, since there was no possible gainful employment, we started organizing performance evenings. Olav Merilo and I sang solos with Mrs.

Triik's accompaniment" (Mägi, 1996:52). Reminiscing about how singing with the choir made her feel, Aino Mägi said,

> I don't remember how many singers we had, but on the stage, we filled two rows. Our first song was "Lenda, lenda lepalind" (Fly, Fly alder bird). The next time we were taken to the dance with the army trucks, we decided to present our songs before the dancing began. Usually we had four songs. Those performances were quite memorable. The soldiers were seated on benches in the hall. The stage was lit. We were ready in rows behind the stage. When the hall was quiet, we walked on to the stage, first the back row then the first. The minute the first girls appeared, the applause and whistling started. We were all dressed in makeshift folk costumes. When the choir was on stage, I stepped to the front, wearing a borrowed white silk embroidered long-sleeved blouse and a northern Estonian skirt with colorful stripes on white background. All the songs were light and melodious where the words did not really matter. These we performed for the British soldiers on weekends before the dancing began.
>
> (Mägi, 1996:51)

Figure 3.1 Alt Garge mixed choir, director Aino Mägi in front row, fifth from the left

This was still a time of transition. Estonians were being moved around to different camps as the UNRRA tried to combine ethnic groups together. Estonians who had left their homeland at different times from their family members moved from location to location, trying to find their families. Aino Mägi recounted how the choirs would evolve as singers moved around to different camps:

> We got addition to this camp, by Mrs. Treek a soloist from Tartu and a good pianist. She started to give me singing lessons and Olav Merilo, a tenor. This camp was closed, and Mr. Ottan and Mrs. Treek went to different camps. Wherever I moved I kept our choir singing.
>
> (Mägi interview, 1991)

Aino Mägi moved to the Oxford DP camp near Dannenberg in Northern Germany and was again a choir director (Figure 3.2). Her birthday celebration in the Oxford camp was a special memory for her:

> I knew that the choir members would come at twelve midnight to wake me up with singing. For that I needed the birthday kringel,

Figure 3.2 Oxford mixed choir, director Aino Mägi in front row, fifth from the left

pretzel-shaped sweet bread with raisins. The barracks had no kitchens; all food was cooked in the common kitchen in the mess hall. I had obtained a half a pound of butter, but nothing else.

Pühapäeval, 2. oktoobril 1949, kell 19.00

G r e v e n i s

K O O R I K O N T S E R T

Kaastegevad: Lingeni Eesti Segakoor,
juh. Aug. Ruut
A. Mägi (sopran)
L. Meigo (bass)
Klaveril: A. Pohla

K a v a

I

1. A. LÄTE — Laul Röömule
   E. VÕRK — Lilleside
   M. HÄRMA — Veel kaitse kange Kalev
   M. HÄRMA — Tule koju
   E. OJA — Kangakudumise laul
   J. AAVIK — Meie laulame

   Segakoor

2. Rahvaviis — Kus on kurva kodu
   G. ERNESAKS — Hulkur

   Hr. L. Meigo

II

3. T. VETTIK — Teid ma tervitan
   J. AAVIK — Kodutee
   E. OJA — Kägu kukub
   R. PÄTS — Pulmalaul
   A. VEDRO — Midrilinnu mäng

   Segakoor

4. J. MANDRE — Kodunõmm
   O. MERIKANTO — Päike paistab

   Pr. A. Mägi

5. E. AAV — Laulik
   E. MELNGAILIS — Tutiline linnukene
   J. JÜRME — Rukkirääk

   Segakoor

- - o o O O O o o - -

Figure 3.3 Lingen program featuring soloist Aino Mägi

> I went to the camp cook Mrs. Lepik with my dilemma to plead for help. She was willing to help but said that I had not enough butter. There was no way to get any more. The cook was an exceptionally kind person. She thought for a minute and promised to see what she can do. In the evening, a large golden-brown kringel arrived at my barrack. Mrs. Lepik's food was always tasty regardless of the minimal rations. Midnight arrived. From behind the door we heard the song 'Why are you drowsy and sleep so long?' The party lasted into the early morning hours, singing choral and other popular songs.
>
> (Mägi, 1996:53)

Mägi next moved to Lingen in 1948 and joined a choir there: "By that time there was a lot of musical activity in camps. Artists came to perform in Lingen, and I was able to copy solo music from them and perform" (Mägi, 1996:54). These concerts included soloists as well as the mixed choirs. They sang many concerts, including one on July 2, 1949, to commemorate the 80th anniversary of the first Estonian song festival (Figure 3.3).

Program translation:

Lingen Estonian High School
Saturday, July 2, 1949 8 PM
Concert
First Estonian Song festival
80th Jubilee

Contributing: L. Kopli-Wiegandt (mezzo-soprano)

A. Mägi (soprano)
L. Meigo (baritone)
Lingen Estonian Mixed Choir, directed by A. Ruut

Program

I

1. Avasõna (opening)	J. Lepik
2. Kõne (greeting)	Mari Raamot
3. A. LÄTE	Laul rõõmule (song of joy)
E. AAV	Laulik (singer)
M. HÄRMA	Veel kaitse kange Kalev (still protect mighty Kalev)
M. HÄRMA	Tule koju (Come home)

II

4. M. Lüdig	Lapsepõlves (in childhood)

J. Mandre	Kodunömm (meadow home) Mrs. Mägi
5. G. Ernesaks	Hulkur (vagabond)
A. Läte	Kuldrannake (gold coast)
	Mr. L. Meigo
6. K. Tuvike	Ööbikule (to the nightingale)
Rahvalaul	Mu meelen (remembering my golden home)
	Mrs. L. Kopli-Wiegandt
7. J. Aavik	Avalaul (opening song)
R. Päts	Labajala valss (flat foot waltz)
E. Melugaitis	Tutiline linnukene (tufted bird)
V. Nerep	Saarlaste laul (Saaremaa islanders' song)
	Segakoor (mixed choir)

The British zone UNRRA supported the Lübeck Men's Choir in several tours of DP camps. Transportation included walking, trucks, and trains as these men sang around Germany from 1945 to 1947 (Figures 3.4 and 3.5).

The DP camp at Geislingen an der Steige was much larger than Lingen and soon had multiple choirs. In 1948 its rosters included:

> *Segakoor* (mixed choir): 28 sopranos, 21 altos, 13 tenors, 12 basses
> *Naiskoor* (women's choir) (also members of the mixed choir): 6 first sopranos, 6 second sopranos, 6 first altos, 5 second altos
> *Eesti Meeslaulu Selts* (Estonian men's choir club): 80 men's voices

Figure 3.4 Lübek men's choir boarding Hamburg train

43 Eesti Meeslaulu Selts, Geislingen, reisimas

Figure 3.5 Eesti Meeslaulu Selts (Estonian Men's Choir) at train station

The "Eesti Meeslaulu Selts" (Estonian men's choir club) in Geislingen was directed by Roman Toi with Walter Loigu as assistant director. One member was Walter's brother, Valdeko Loigu, who went on to become a well-known composer in the United States, receiving the Freedom Foundation Award at Valley Forge for his composition of "Our Good American Home" (Figure 3.6).

The Geislingen mixed choir "Runo" was formed November 14, 1945. By 1948 the choir, directed by Udo Kasemets, had 75 members, 14 who had emigrated (no longer there to sing, but still considered members), eight *sõprusliikmed* (friends of the choir), and one honorary member, Voldemar Päts. The women's choir was formed in 1948 with 23 members, most of whom were also in the mixed choir. One member of both the mixed choir and the women's choir was Maie (Ellen) Rebane (Figure 3.7). Her son remembers,

> My mother had a good singing voice, [she] immediately joined a choir or two, and wanted to train her voice for opera (she was a mezzo soprano). Throughout the tight quarters of the camp one could always hear someone practicing operatic scales and trills, which drove some neighbors up the wall.
>
> (Rebane, 2013:5)

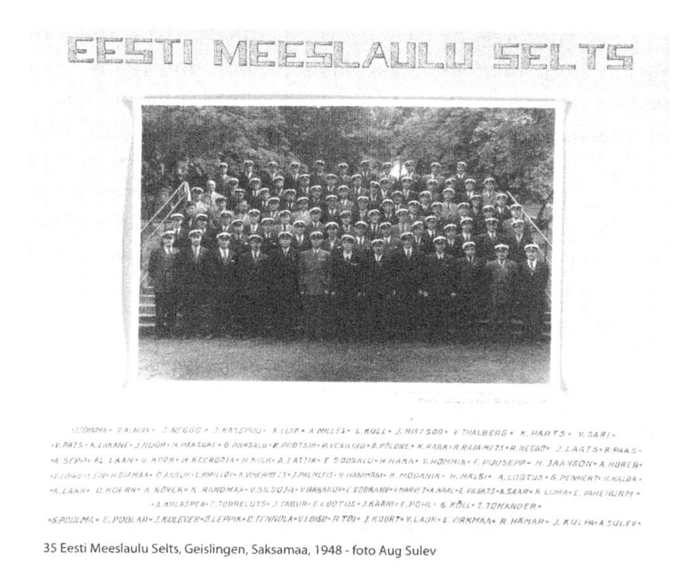

EESTI MEESLAULU SELTS
35 Eesti Meeslaulu Selts, Geislingen, Saksamaa, 1948 - foto Aug Sulev

Figure 3.6 Eesti Meeslaulu (Estonian Men's Choir) in Geislingen

Figure 3.7 Geislingen choir singing at 1946 Summer Days

The Geislingen choirs sponsored the Eesti Suvepäevad (Estonian Summer Days) August 2–4, 1946, at the Jaanhalle. This event included theater productions of *Pygmalion*, *Pisuhuhänd*, and the operetta *Mariza*. Folk dance groups from Estonia, Latvia, and Lithuania performed, and *naisvõimlejate* (women's rhythmic gymnastics) events and sports were held. H. Liudemanse directed a concert by a Latvian mixed choir. The final event was a choral concert of the Estonian men's, women's, and mixed choir music directed by Anton Kasemets, Adelbert Virkhaus, Roman Toi, Meeme Mälgi, and E. Reebs. While this event was not a full *laulupidu*, it had many of the important elements of a song festival and brought great hope to the Estonian refugees (Figure 3.8).

Figure 3.8 Eesti Suvepäevad (Estonian Summer Days) in Geislingen (IHRCA document)

Several thousand displaced Estonians were housed in Augsburg-Hochfeld, which was a large camp with both a mixed choir and a women's choir. Augsburg is a well-established town about 65 miles from Geislingen. Hochfeld is a suburb of Augsburg that housed a large Estonian DP camp. The camp choir was founded as soon as refugees arrived there in the summer of 1945. Meta Noorkukk was the initial choir director of the mixed choir in Augsburg, comprising 45 members. They also had a women's choir with 21 members, directed by Marta Kaasik. Another large DP camp with several thousand Estonians was in Lübek. This camp had a mixed choir with 40 members, directed by August Ruut, as well as a men's choir (Figure 3.9).

Many camps had smaller numbers of Estonians. Viktor Valk was an Estonian prisoner of war in Russia who found his way to Osnabruch, where Latvians and Estonians were housed in the British Zone. Although there were only 100 Estonians in that camp, they "needed singers for the National Day festivals," so a choir was started. Valk had been in school choir and had sung as a soloist, so he joined right in. He was one of the first Estonians to receive transit in 1947 to Australia. His experience in the DP camp choir helped him join the Estonian men's choir that traveled together to Australia (Valk interview, 2008).

Figure 3.9 Lübek men's choir

Near Lübeck, the Flensburg camp held both Latvians and Estonians. The Estonian men's choir there was a tight-knit and very active group. Between August 1945 and June 1947, they toured and performed 55 concerts, including many at major Estonian DP camps at Geislingen, Augsburg, Altenstadt, and Oldenburg (Alet, 1945, Turner notes).

The small camp at Bamberg had a modest mixed choir and a men's quartet. The choir was started by Leida Räga and was later directed by Anton Kasemets, one of the head directors at the 1947 Augsburg Song Festival. This city housed the UNRRA Headquarters as well, so the choir was able to perform there for the local Estonians as well as administrators. They held solo concerts and organ concerts as well as a choir concerts.

Some of the mixed Baltic camps had combined choirs. Los Angeles Estonian choir director Jaak Kukk was in Amberg, where two-thirds of the 100 voices in the choir were Latvians. The choir was directed by Dr. Aberle, a Latvian composition professor. They sang songs in both Estonian and Latvian. There were no Estonian songs available except in an old-fashioned songbook that someone had brought along. Kukk arranged those songs for SATB—soprano, alto, tenor, bass—and wrote other scores from memory for the choir (Kukk, 1995, 2008).

Edgar Siimpoeg had been a French-horn student in the Tallinn Conservatory when World War II broke out. He was conscripted into the German army at age 18 and escaped to work for a German farmer as the war ended. He found his way to the DP camp in Bayern Recht. His first day there, "[t]his redhead I knew from the fourth form as a pianist with stubby fingers, but real good, says, 'We've got a concert tonight. You've got to sing.' So, I sang a lullaby with choir 'Linuka Vaike'" (Siimpoeg interview, 2008). Siimpoeg auditioned and got into the Bavarian Symphony, which became his full-time job during the DP camp years while living in Bayerreucht. The Estonians in Bayerreucht wanted to have a men's choir at the camp, so Siimpoeg recruited the members: "I just said, 'you, you, you, you.' They had all been in the army and I had a few stripes on my shoulder. I would say, 'It doesn't matter you don't sing, I'll teach you to sing'" (Siimpoeg interview, 2008). These men later immigrated together to Australia, where they continued to sing with one another.

Altenstadt, another smaller camp with about 700 Estonians, had a mixed choir started by Roman Toi. Elvi Urv remembers that "Toi was so charismatic everyone followed him. He was a composer and wanted more so he moved to Geislingen where everyone important went. After Toi left, there was not as much choir activity" (Urv, E. interview, 1995) (Figure 3.10).

57 Altenstadt, Eesti Segakoor 1948

Figure 3.10 Altenstadt mixed choir, Roman Toi, director, front row, eighth from the right. Women are wearing matching dresses that they made from surplus war parachutes with hand-embroidered traditional Estonian designs

Companies also organized choirs in some German cities. The Eesti Insenerikompanii (Estonian Engineer Company) and 8090 Lab. Service Company were both men's choirs from Frankfurt that performed at the 1947 Augsburg Song Festival.

School music in the camps

Estonian children attended schools while they were living in the DP camps. Parents were particularly interested in choirs as they provided education and the chance to promote the Estonian identity for their children (Vesilind interview, 2014). One group calling themselves the Geislingen Yugend (Geislingen children) still gather from many countries to share their common heritage. Mai Maddison edited and published a book describing their memories of that time as young children (Maddison, 2015). The story of the Geislingen school children is also told in the film "Coming Home Soon" by Helge Merits (2018), available on DVD.

Each Estonian school included music lessons and choir as part of the curriculum. Arved Plaks remembers learning to sing parts from his friend Taavo Virkhaus so they could "hum parts in class. We did this to tease the geography teacher. We were part of the 'Geislingen Yugend' with Alan Lehtiste and Gunnar Auksi, We sang 'Meil aia ääres tänaval.' We still get together at Estonian days" (Plaks interview, 2008). They were part of the Geislingen High School choir, as everyone in the school was expected to join. There was only one piano in the Geislingen school, so the choir had to rehearse after all music classes and lessons were complete, from 9 to 10 p.m. The choir had people arriving mid-year and others leaving as they received permission to emigrate. Still, they were able to put on a concert at the end of each year, attended by most of the Geislingen Estonian community.

Having started high school choir in Hanover in 1947, then Kempten in 1948, and finally in Geislingen in 1948, Inno Salasoo remembers that the music was handwritten and later mimeographed. He saved some of that handwritten music, which can be seen in this book. Salasoo sang with the basses on Virkhaus' cantata. In this cantata the bass is very high because "it's supposed to sound painful and needy" (Salasoo interview, 1996). Each of these Estonian refugee high schoolers went on to sing in Estonian choirs and song festivals as part of the Estonian diaspora around the world.

Schools benefited from the many professional musicians. Martin's memoirs about the high school in Geislingen explain, "For example Udo Kasemets, who is a rather well-known Estonian composer now, often directed our choir and also taught music at our *gümnaasium* there" (Martin, 2009:82). The choir directors at Geislingen high school also included Aavo Virkhaus (uncle of Taavo) and Anton Kasemets, who had quite a rivalry as the local conductors, and both conducted at the Augsburg Song Festival in 1947.

Transit camp choirs

Refugees who were approved for emigration left the DP camps and went to temporary "transit camps" as they awaited their eventual departure to Australia, Canada, England, and the USA. Even in these small units, choirs were formed to sing while they waited for the boats to take them far away. Of the 1948 Münster transit camp with about 100 Estonians, Raivo Kalamäe (interview 2008) remembers, "We had a little choir with 16 members of four each soprano, alto, tenor, bass." A bass named Pomerants knew the tunes and taught them to the group. They had choir practice in the evening and sang for national days. Kalamäe later emigrated to Australia and sang in Sydney's Estonian mixed choir and men's choir.

Choirs were quickly formed in all the Estonian camps. To help coordinate activities, the Estonians in the American Zone formed the Eesti Kooride Keskus (EKK, Estonian Choral Center) to coordinate activities between camps. At the time of the group's formation in 1945, there were choirs known to be performing in 20 DP camps, including Miltenberg, Augsburg-Hochfeld, Geislingen, Altenstadt, Gunzenhausen, and Wiesbaden. The EKK board included chair Roman Toi, Emil Eerme, J. Juhanso, Adalbert Virkhaus, Meeme Mälgi, P. Mutt, and H. Roonurm.

With so many Estonian choirs spread all over the British and American zones in post-war Germany, it is no surprise that they longed for song festivals as a familiar, communal form of camaraderie, creativity, and optimism. Song festivals give singers a goal to work toward—something much needed in the camps. The traditional *laulupidu* (song festival) presents the best side of Estonians to the world, another value that was important to those in the camps. With refugees scattered across Germany, a song festival would provide a way to get together with friends and family. The goals became clear, and many Estonians were eager to be part of the preparations. Amid great expectations, the plans for the 1947 Augsburg Song Festival began.

4 Welcome to the singing party!

The 1947 Augsburg song festival

Displaced Estonians knew how important the song festivals had been in the past to their people. The festivals had historically helped in times of foreign rule:

> *Eriti olulist tähtsust omasid esimesed laulupeod, mis toimusid võõraste võimukandjate survevalitsuste ajastul. Laulupidude läbi süttis eesti rahvas rahvuslik enesetunne, laulupeod kinnitasid usku eesti rahva vaimujõusse ja eluõigusse ning julgustasid ja ergutasid võitluseks rahvuslike ja riiklike õiguste eest.*
>
> (Particularly important were the first song festivals that took place in the era of foreign rulers. Through song festivals, the Estonian people ignited a sense of nationality, the song festivals affirmed their faith in the spiritual power and life of the Estonian people and encouraged them to fight for nation and national rights.)
>
> (translation of Eesti Pagulaste Laulupidu—Estonian Refugee Song festival notes from committee, August 10, 1947)

Under the controlling eye of the Soviet Union, an Estonian song festival was being prepared for Tallinn in 1947. At the same time, plans were being developed for an Estonian song festival in Augsburg, Germany, for the displaced Estonians.

With so many DP camps in Germany after WWII, a significant number of refugees were trying to locate their family and friends. One way to do that was to participate in activities that brought together communities from different camps, such as sports events and music concerts. Both types of activities were sponsored by the UNRRA and the British and American armies. The US Army in particular "wanted to keep spirits of the refugees high so they did very nice things like provide the transportation with their army convoy trucks" (Liivi Joe email, 2008). One of the events sponsored by the UNRRA in the

American Zone was the 1947 Augsburg Song Festival. This sponsorship meant providing help with transportation as well as supplies in limited amounts.

Preparing for the song festival

With such clear needs for a festival, many Estonians were willing and ready to help organize one. The UNRRA required that each community have governing groups within their DP camp. Out of these, the organizing committees for song festivals were formed. The 1947 song festival booklet listed the organizing committee members:

> Eesti Kooride Keskuse Juhtus (Estonian Choral Central Committee) Chair Anton Kasemets, members: Marta Kaasik, P. Lüdig, Rein Neggo, E. Rajamets, Roman Toi and A. Virkhaus
>
> Laulupeo üldtoimkond (song festival main committee) Chair: Aksel Luitsalu, members: E. Juhansoo, Marta Kaasik, Anton Kasemets, S Kelder, A. Lennu, A. Raag, V. Solom, Roman Toi, A. Tõnisson, J. Varend, Alice Viilup, Mari Ülper
>
> Kassa ja büroo (tickets, business): J. Varen, E. Goeschel
>
> Majutamine (finding lodging): A. Tönisson, S. Kelder
>
> Toitlustamine (food): Mari Ülper, Erika Ploompuu Alice Viilup
>
> Korrapidamine (maintaining order): V. Solom, J. Pleer
>
> Külaliste vastuvötmine ja informatsioon (reception and information): A. Lannu, E. Juhansoo
>
> Esmaabi (first aid): Hochfeld ambulance group
>
> (list from 1947 *Augsburg Laulupidu kava*—Augsburg Song Festival program available in IHRCA and Estonian Archives in Sydney Australia)

Meetings were held and supplies were gathered at the Laulupeo büroo (song festival bureau) office, which was housed in the schoolhouse at Hochfeldstrasse 60. Hochfeld is a suburb of Augsburg and contained a large Estonian DP camp; it was also near Geislingen, the largest of the Estonian DP camps.

One of the first items of business was to get the word out to other choirs. The usual lines of communication were completely disrupted by their relocation to Germany, but this needed to happen quickly for choirs to get music prepared to sing together. The Kassa ja büroo (tickets, business) group began to reach out to choirs in other camps. Augsburg was very close to Geislingen, so the directors from Geislingen were probably in on the song festival plans from the beginning. A postal service had been established by the UNRRA, so announcements could be sent to other Estonian camps. The Estonian newspapers published in the larger DP camps, such as *Eesti Rada* in Augsburg and *Eesti Post* in Geislingen, ran announcements and provided contact information. While there was obviously limited telecommunication, strong social networking was in place to communicate between camps. Estonians who had moved from camp to camp already had contacts in other choirs as well as family members who would help spread the word.

The head conductors (Roman Toi, Udo Kasemets, Anton Kasemets, and August Pruul) needed to choose the repertoire to begin rehearsals for the combined choir numbers, and that music selection would need to be disseminated to the visiting choirs. No official choir books could be printed for the festival. Each choir would need to figure out how to learn the complex choral compositions that would be in the concert. This involved borrowing and hand-copying choir scores.

Song festivals include more than just the choral concerts. There are other events to prepare. The 1947 Augsburg Song Festival committee invited soloists to perform in a recital for the festival. They decided to invite four well-known Estonian musicians from Blomberg in the British Zone; they would need to be contacted and arrangements would need to be made for them to rehearse together in the local theater. Theater groups were prevalent in the Estonian DP camps, so naturally these groups were also invited to perform. Many Estonians had free time in the camps that allowed much artistic expression to flow. An art show that featured Estonian folk art and contemporary art was prepared to display the Estonian visual culture.

The song festival committee needed to find a good space for the event. The featured concert needed to be outdoors with room for a large choir (720 voices) and a large audience (5,000). The outdoor stage chosen was a lovely venue in Augsburg near the Hochfeld region. It is still used as a theater in Augsburg and is known as the *Freilichtbühne am Roten Tor* (Outdoor Stage at Red Gate).

Spaces were also needed for rehearsals, registration and hospitality, an art and book show, theater, and the soloist concert. These were most likely in the Hochfeld area of Augsburg as that is where the Estonian DP camp was located. The Messerschmitt Nazi plane factory and other arms factories had been in Hochfeld. The barracks that held the many forced laborers had been converted into a DP camp. This area included some common spaces that could be used for the art and book show and for choir rehearsals.

Every Estonian song festival has a parade, so of course the Augsburg event included one as well. Next, a route for a parade to the song festival opening was planned and prepared. The plan was to have the parade start at the Hochfeld train station where many guests would arrive. There is no longer a station at this site, though the Augsburg Railway Park is currently in that location. The parade would go from the station along Hochfeldstrasse for two kilometers to the song festival grounds at the Red Gate.

Accommodating visiting choirs presented another important and complex challenge. Housing would be needed for choir members for the evening after the rehearsal day, August 9, 1947, and for August 10, the evening after the festival. Families were already living in tightly packed spaces with four to eight in a room. Friends and family would take in those whom they knew. Some makeshift quarters could be made in the old barracks in Hochfeld. The Bavarian warm weather in August would likely make simple housing easier to establish, and everyone had been through a string of temporary housing situations during and after the war, so they were quite adaptable. The many Estonians and locals coming for the festival day as audience members would be expected to find their own accommodations.

Providing food was a constant worry for everyone in post-war Germany. Meals had to be prepared with minimal rations. Estonian song festival hosts traditionally feed choir members soup (most often vegetable or split pea) and rye bread for lunch and dinner. That is most likely what was available in 1947—albeit with a much thinner soup and only one small slice of bread without butter.

Knowing that there would be an extra 5,000 people in for the festival meant storing up extra medical supplies. The first aid committee was headed by some of the many Estonian medical professionals who were refugees. Walking the parade route and standing for hours in the choir would be difficult for people who had limited food rations. Water and food would be an important part of the first aid station.

The tickets and business committee and the reception and information committee needed to find supplies before the festival. Sources of funding for these supplies also needed to be found. Some of the scarce paper allowed for administration at the camp could be stockpiled for tickets and programs. Other sources needed to be found to cover this much printing. Support from the UNRRA was very helpful at this point. The actual printing of tickets and programs was done in Geislingen, where the Estonian community had their own printing facility set up by 1947.

Ticket prices for concerts and the theater were planned and tickets printed. The ticket prices were in RM (German marks) and needed to cover costs, while still being affordable. The head of the ticket committee reported,

> Laulupeo pääsmed istekohtadele olid Üldtoimkonna poolt määratud köik ühehinnaliseks, nimelt RM 5 mis vörreldud tolleaegse rahakursiga polnud mitte kallis kui arvestada, et pakk ameerika sigarette samal ajal maksis mustalt ca 70 RM. Mitmehinnaliste piletite müügil poleks olnud ka mingit erilist tähtsust, sest nähtavus ning kuuldavus oli kogu kuulajaskonna tribüünil peaaegu vördne, kui mitte keskmistes ja tagumistes ridades ei olnud parem.
>
> (The singing party seating was all priced by the General Committee, namely RM 5, which was not expensive compared to the money of the time, considering that a pack of American cigarettes cost about RM 70 at the same time on the black market. Selling multi-priced tickets would not have been of much importance, as visibility and audibility on the grandstand as a whole were almost equal, if not in the middle and rear rows.)
>
> (*Eesti Pagulaste Laulupidu*, Augsburg, August 10, 1947)

The song festival had an elaborate music program that was prepared by the committee under the direction of Head Choral Director, Anton Kasemets. The printed program cover artwork and emblem for the festival were created by Peet Aren (1898–1970). Aren was a well-known artist in Estonia who created many wonderful watercolor, sketches, and graphic art works. The festival emblem featured a *kannel* (Estonian zither) amid oak leaves. Both are beloved symbols of Estonian culture. The program also included biographies of the four chief choir directors, the program order for both days' events, song lyrics, a list of participating choirs, and a short history of Estonian song festivals from 1869 to that date (Figure 4.1).

Figure 4.1 "Estonian refugees song festival in Germany 1947 August 10th in Augsburg" (program cover from IHRCA).

The program booklet listed the scheduled events including:
Saturday, August 9, 1947:

3:00 PM	Soloists concert at Ludwigshaus featuring Liidia Aadre (soprano), Carmen Prii-Berendsen (violin), Karin Prii-Raudsepp (piano) and Naatan Pöld (tenor).
6:00 PM	Mixed choir rehearsal, Hochfeld Camp
9:00 PM	Men's Choir and Women's Choir rehearsal at Hochfeld Camp

Sunday, August 10, 1947:

7:00 AM	Women's and Men's Choir dress rehearsals at song stage
8:00 AM	Mixed choir dress rehearsal at song stage
9:00 AM	Geislingen ERK theater group presents "Põrgupõhja Uus Vanapagan" by A.H. Tammsaare at Ludwigshaus
1:30 PM	Parade from Hochfeld train station to festival site
2:00 PM	Combined choir concert "Freilichtspiele" (Open-air Games) with 18 choirs and 720 singers directed by Anton Kasemets, Udo Kasemets, August Pruul, and Roman Toi

Song Festival program order:

Opening song "Üks Kindral Linn ja Varjupaik" (A Mighty Fortress is Our God)
Opening words by Estonian Choir Chair P. Lüdig
Speech by Professor E. Ein
Greetings from many groups
Concert by combined choirs
Closing words by Song Festival chair A. Luitsalu

As the song festival neared, rehearsals were held in each town to prepare the music. Time for rehearsals at the festival would be very limited and could only be used to work on balance and familiarizing the choir with the acoustics of the space. The head conductors visited some of the other DP camps to help with detailed rehearsals and communicated information about their interpretations of the compositions. Preparing for the song festival involved considerable effort and coordination among many parties.

At last, the song festival begins!

After months of preparation, the party began. Estonians arrived from other DP camps as singers, art sellers, actors, dignitaries, and audience members. At the Augsburg train station, a banner read "Tähelepanu, tähelepanu, eestlased! Teretulemast Augsburgi laulupeole! Omnibus ootab teid jaama väljapääsu juures…" (Attention, attention, Estonians! Welcome to the Augsburg Singing Party! The Omnibus is waiting for you at the station's exit…). As the song festival opened, the many events began that were arranged in conjunction with the festival. An art exhibit included hand-carved Estonian beer mugs, jewelry, boxes, pictures, plates, and vases for sale. There were Estonian language books and newspapers for purchase. Some sold were books brought by the refugees; others were books printed in the DP camps. As Estonians browsed the festival shops, they found friends and relatives who had come from other camps and were happily reunited (Figures 4.2–4.4).

Figure 4.2 Art exhibit items from Augsburg Song Festival, hand-carved wooden Estonian beer mug, picture, box, and pin (photo E. Soovere).

Figure 4.3 Reading the news at the Augsburg Song Festival Bookstore (photo by E. Soovere).

Figure 4.4 Augsburg Song Festival bookstore (photo by E. Soovere).

On August 9, 1947, at three o'clock—the first afternoon of the festival—the Soloists' Concert was presented. Many talented Estonian professional musicians had escaped from Soviet-controlled Estonia at the end of WWII, including two sisters, violinist Carmen Prii-Berendsen and pianist Karin Prii-Raudsepp, as well as singers Liidia Aadre and Naatan Põld (Figure 4.5–4.7). All four were in the Blomberg DP camp in the British Zone. The soloists' program included all-Estonian compositions:

Rudolf Tobias (1873–1918) Sonatina
Allegro
Adagio molto cantabile
Allegro vivace
Performed by Karin Prii-Raudsepp on piano

Mihkel Lüdig (1880 and that time still living in Estonia, died in 1958)
Minu Altar (my altar)
Alfred Karindi (1901 at that time still living, died 1969)
Hällilaul (Lullaby)
Tuudur Vettik (1898, at that time still living in Estonia, died 1982)
Merella on sinine (The sea is blue)
Eduard Oja (1905, still living at the time in Estonia, died 1950)
Põhjamaa lapsed (Nordic Children)
Performed by Naatan Põld, tenor

Heino Eller (1887, living at that time, died 1970)
Sonaat (1922)
Performed by Carmen Prii-Berendsen, violin and
Karin Prii-Raudsepp, piano

Intermission

Tuudur Vettik (1898–1982)
Sügislinnule (For the Autumn Bird)
Evald Aav (1900–1939)
Ainult palve (Only prayer)
Juhan Aavik (1884, living in Sweden at that time, died 1982)
Kojuigatsus (Longing for Home)
Mart Saar (1882, living at that time in Estonia, died 1969)
Tuule Hölmas (In the arms of the wind)
Performed by Liidia Aadre, Soprano

Eduard Tubin (1905, living at that time in Sweden, died 1982)
Meditatsioon
Heino Eller (1887–1970) Männid (Pinet)
Eduard Oja (1905–1950) Magatsitlite tants "Aeliita-süidist"
(Magri's dance from "Aellita Suite"
Performed by Carmen Prii-Berendsen, violin and
Karin Prii-Raudsepp, piano
Evald Aav (1900–1939) Kaks aariat ja duett oop. "Vikerlased"
(two arias and duet from the opera "Vikerlased" [The Vikings])
Performed by Naatan Põld, tenor and Liidia Aadre, soprano

Figure 4.5 Violin soloist Carmen Prii-Berendsen performing at Augsburg 1947 Song Festival (photo E. Epner).

Figure 4.6 Piano soloist Karin Prii-Raudsepp performing at Augsburg 1947 Song Festival (photo E. Epner).

Figure 4.7 Soprano soloist Liidia Aadre and tenor soloist Naatan Pöld performing at Augsburg 1947 Song Festival (photo E. Epner).

After the soloists' concert, there was a 6 p.m. mixed choir rehearsal at Hochfeld Camp, followed by 9 p.m. men's choir and women's choir rehearsals at Hochfeld Camp. The choirs had already learned the songs thoroughly, and so this was a chance just to sing for joy as they reunited with friends and family who had lived through some extremely trying times. No words could contain how they felt, so this was an amazing chance to breathe as one. Singing together there must have been an overwhelming and joyous experience.

Early the next morning, the men's and women's choirs held a 7 a.m. rehearsal on the song festival stage. This was primarily to get familiar with the acoustics of this outdoor stage. Most of the singers were also in the mixed choir, so they stayed for that 8 a.m. rehearsal on the same stage. These rehearsals were held early, as no one wanted to miss the theater production.

The theater production of *Põrgupõhja Uus Vanapagan* (*Hell's New Old Damn*, sometimes translated as *Hell's New Old Pagan*), by Estonian author A. H. Tammsaare, was presented in the Ludwigshaus at 9 a.m. The play is based on the 1939 novel also by Tammsaare. This was a new work at the time, dealing with peasant life via multi-layered political, theological, and cultural issues. It is still a popular play and was made into Estonian-language films in 1964 and 1976 (Figure 4.8).

Figure 4.8 Theater production at Augsburg 1947 Song Festival (photo by E. Soovere).

Figure 4.9 Parade Maypoles open the parade in the Augsburg 1947 Song Festival (photo E. Epner).

The song festival parade started at 1:30 p.m. with a route that went from the Hochfeld train station (the current Augsburg train park) to the festival grounds. All 720 singers and many children and dignitaries lined up in the procession to the festival. Many wore traditional Estonian folk costumes that they had carried with them from Estonia or that they had managed to create from materials that they could find locally. Along the route, the many audience members were there to cheer them on. The Augsburg parade began at 1:30 p.m., with maypoles carried by children. The middle of the maypole showed the song festival emblem with the kannel and oak leaves designed by Peet Aren (Figure 4.9).

Next came the Head Conductors, Roman Toi, Udo Kasemets, Anton Kasemets, and August Pruul, dressed in their fine, crisp tuxedos. These would have been difficult items of clothing to find in a DP camp. Roman Toi explained that he had exchanged cigarettes

Figure 4.10 Parade entrance of Head Conductors from left to right: Roman Toi, August Pruul, Anton Kasemets, Udo Kasemets (photo E. Epner).

with local Germans to find a tuxedo for his role in the event. All four wore Head Conductor badges with the song festival emblem, which were handmade for them by the local song festival committee (Figure 4.10).

The Head Conductors were followed by the eighteen choirs with their choir directors. Like the Head Conductors, all of the choir directors wore badges made for the festival. Most of the women wore traditional Estonian folk costumes from the regions of their families. One of the choirs had costumes made from surplus war parachutes with traditional Estonian embroidery. Some of the men had traditional Estonian costumes or wore suits. One of the men's choirs had members wearing American army uniforms, including hats and shoes that were given to them for doing extra labor for the United States army (Figures 4.11–4.13).

As they reached the stage, the choirs took their places, and the directors came to the front row (Figure 4.14).

Figure 4.11 Altenstadt choir with surplus war parachute dresses in Augsburg parade (photo E. Epner).

Figure 4.12 Choir with army uniforms in Augsburg parade (photo E. Epner).

Figure 4.13 1947 Song Festival parade along Hochfeldstrasse in Augsburg, Germany (photo E. Epner, Mikelson collection).

Figure 4.14 Song Festival head choir directors reaching platform at the Outdoor Stage at Red Door, Augsburg (photo E. Epner, Mikelson collection).

The song festival program

The two-kilometer walk for the entire group to get from the station to the stage took around half an hour. The song festival began at 2:15 p.m. with a trumpet fanfare, and then an orchestra played with the combined choirs singing "Üks kindle linn ja varjupaik" (A Mighty Fortress is Our God). Next there was an opening presentation by the Deputy Chairman of the Estonian Choir Center, P. Lüdig, and, following that, a speech by Professor Ernst Ein, Chairman of the American Zone Estonian Central Committee (Figure 4.15).

The audience was large and enthusiastic. Describing the audiences of earlier song festivals held in Estonia, choir director Mägis explained,

> For the first song festivals almost half of Estonian people went to these. Our mind we wanted to do something that satisfied our minds. We are not satisfied just physically. We had to learn or achieve something more to get satisfaction. What gave most satisfaction didn't cost anything—was singing.
>
> (Mägi, 1991)

In the DP camps, it was also important to each Estonian that they go to the festival, if at all possible, whether they sang or were in the

Figure 4.15 Ernst Ein, Chairman of the American Zone Estonians, speaking at opening ceremony (photo E. Epner).

Figure 4.16 Audience at the Augsburg 1947 Song Festival at the *Freilicht-bühne am Roten Tor* (photo E. Epner).

audience. The audience of 5,000 were all dressed in the finest clothing they could find or borrow. Looking across this audience, one would not imagine these people were refugees. Every effort was made to look one's best for this momentous occasion (Figure 4.16).

A key function of the program was to present Estonian culture to the rest of Europe. Officials were invited from other Baltic DP groups and speeches were made in other languages. The interpretation for speakers on the program was provided by Estonian high school English teacher Elga Mikelson, who translated from Estonian, Latvian, Lithuanian, and German into English, since this was in the American Zone of Germany (Figures 4.17 and 4.18).

The choral portion of the program began with the combined mixed choirs, which brought 555 voices together in song. The first half of the program included eight Estonian compositions and one Finnish composition. The four head directors took turns leading these pieces (Figures 4.19 and 4.20).

The second half of the program started with the 102 singers of the combined women's choirs, who performed four Estonian songs under the direction of August Pruul. Next, the 285-voice combined men's choir performed, singing six Estonian songs under the direction of Roman Toi (Figure 4.21).

Figure 4.17 Elga Mikelson translating for Augsburg Song Festival (photo by E. Epner).

Figure 4.18 Elga Mikelson translating for Augsburg Song Festival Committee Chair, Aksel Luitsalu (photo E. Epner).

Figure 4.19 Mixed choir singing at the 1947 Augsburg Song Festival (E. Epner).

Figure 4.20 Directors and audience in the *Freilichtbühne,* Augsburg, Germany (photo E. Epner).

Figure 4.21 Men's choir in the 1947 Augsburg Song Festival (photo E. Epner).

Figure 4.22 Augsburg 1947 Song Festival Choir Directors with flowers (photo by E. Soovere).

EESTI POST

ESTONIAN NEWSPAPER — „ESTONIAN POST"

Augsburgis kôlas vaba Eesti laul

Figure 4.23 Eesti Post (Estonian Paper) headline "Augsburgis kõlas vaba Eesti laul" (In Augsburg was heard free Estonian song) (IHRCA collection).

Figure 4.24 Choir member in traditional Estonian folk costume at 1947 Augsburg Song Festival (photo E. Epner).

The final seven songs were performed by the combined mixed choirs. The first piece was a Latvian song and the second a Lithuanian song, both sung in Estonian. The group sang four more Estonian songs. The song titles and composers from the Augsburg program are listed in Appendix C. While it was not listed on the program, the choirs did sing "Tuljak," the Estonian wedding song, as an encore, as is done at most Estonian song festivals.

Flowers are traditionally brought to the directors at a song festival. Miraculously flowers were indeed found to bring to the directors at Augsburg (Figure 4.22). Closing words were offered by Aksel Luitsalu, chair of the song festival committee.

The festival was a tremendous success. Articles about the high quality of singing and the hospitality of the Augsburg Estonians were printed in the Estonian DP newspapers *Eesti Rada*, *Kauge Kodu*, and *Eesti Post*. The local German paper *Im Ausland* carried a front-page photo of the Estonian choirs marching with the Estonian flag to the Augsburg outdoor theater. Another photo featured an Estonian singer in her "schönen Volkstracht" (beautiful folk costume) (Figures 4.23 and 4.24).

Such rich documentation of the festival survives in large part thanks to two Estonian photographers, Elmer Epner and Eric Soovere. Amateur photographer Epner shot events with equipment that he had carried with him from Estonia. Film was very difficult to get; something had to be traded (cigarettes, food, or shoes, usually) for it. Epner put together a book of the photos that he showed around to take orders for individual pictures from his negatives. After all the orders were done, Geislingen high school teacher and translator for the festival Elga Mikelson asked for the book, which Epner gave to her. While living in the Augsburg DP camp, Epner wrote a short book, *Estonia: Progress, Achievement, Fate*, translated into English by Mikelson. This book included a photo from the 1947 song festival on the cover and one of the choir photos from the festival, along with many more of Epner's photos from the DP camps. It was published in the Augsburg camp (Epner, 1948). Three DVDs of Epner's film work are held in the IHRCA Collection 3875: "Metro Rhythmics and Harmony in Motion," "The Estonian Heritage," and "Midsummer Holiday." Epner's book of photos of the DP camps, with captions translated by Mikelson, can be seen in digital version at: https://www.digar.ee/arhiiv/nlib-digar:386572.

On the other hand, Eric Soovere (1916–2008) was already a professional photographer when he left Estonia. His account of the 1944 travels with his family from Tartu to Augsburg in a cart through the devastation of Europe are collected in a book and a video that utilizes his stills (Soovere, 1999). He also took photos at the song festival that he gave to Elga Mikelson, which are also used in this book. The local Estonian and German newspapers carried photos by both Epner and Soovere. Some also carried a few photos taken by A. Oja. Many Estonians bought these papers and carried them with them to places where they emigrated. The newspapers are available in the IHRCA archives and in the Australian Estonian archives in Sydney.

Considering the understandable animosity between the Germans who had given up their homes and Estonians who were in a place that they did not want to be, it is particularly significant that the local Germans embraced this song festival. The article in the German newspaper notes, "Die Este und der Gesang sind unzertrennlich. Die alten und aus weiter Vergangenheit stammenden Ueberlieferungen künden davon, dass die Esten immer ein gesangliebendes Volk waren" (Estonians and song are inseparable. The ancient traditions tell us that the Estonians have always been a vocal people) (*Im Ausland* August 1947). Indeed, the Estonian DPs felt buoyed up by the emotional as well as financial success of the festival. The entire festival took in 36,000 RM. Expenses had been 31,000 RM, so 5,000 RM remained to put in the choir fund for the next festival. Soon plans formed for another festival to be held in Kempten, Germany on September 26, 1948, in the great hall of the Kornhaus.

After the festival, the goal of telling Estonia's story seemed to strike a chord with the German journalists. The writer for *Im Ausland* explained that

> Zum Schluss seiner Rede sagte Prof. Ein, dass wohl heute noch über der Freiheit vieler Völker ein tiefes Dunkel laste, doch wir seien alle fest und unerschüttert in dem Glauben, dass dieser Austand nicht ewig wärt, dass auch die Esten wieder einmal in einem freie Staat in der Familie der anderen nordischen Völker einemneuen Freiheitsmorgen entgegengehen würden.
>
> (At the end of his speech, Prof. Ein said that even today the freedom of many peoples still weighs deep and dark, but we are all firm and unshaken in the belief that this exchange would not last forever, that the Estonians would once again live in one free state in the family of other Nordic peoples and would face a new day of freedom.)
>
> (*Im Ausland* August 20, 1947)

These warm thoughts must have been particularly encouraging to the Estonian refugees who still worried that their country might never again be free. This song festival gave strength and resilience to the singers and to the audience.

5 "First I chose songs that everyone knew"

Choir directors, scores, repertoire, and composers in Estonian displaced person camps

The Augsburg Song Festival ended with a song not listed on the program, but one that Estonians had come to expect at cultural celebrations. Since the national song festival in 1934, audiences would clap until "Tuljak" was performed as an encore—perhaps even several times. This tune is very upbeat and spirited, with happy lyrics and a fast tempo. On its face, perhaps "Tuljak" would seem an unusual choice in desperate times for those with little chance of returning home. However, it was just what was needed to raise spirits and give meaning to life. Its tale of falling in love, marrying, and preserving traditions was an important touchstone for resilience and was emblematic of the importance of going on with life.

"Tuljak" is the song most mentioned by all the Estonian interviewees who had sung in the displaced person (DP) camps. In 1946, the Geislingen Mixed Choir placed it on a program, but the traditional tune is not listed either in the 1947 Augsburg program or in the 1948 Kempten material. After Augsburg, the festival committee reported,

> Kui kõnetooli astus üldtoimkonna esimees A. Luitsalu, tegi ta asjatuid katseid lõppsõna ütlemiseks. Üha enam paisusid lainetavalt tormitsevad hüüded: nõuti "Tuljakut". Laulupeo üldjuhid kahtlesid, sest seda laulu polnud kavas ja sellega polnud tehtud ka proove, ent lakkamatult jätkusid hüüded: "Tuljak, tuljak..." Meme sate; astus viimaks juhi kohale: A. Kasemets ning tema juhatusel vaimustas üldkoori jõuline "Tuljak" peokülalisi ja üllatas nii juhatajaid kui ka lauljaid endid.
>
> (When A. Luitsalu, the chairman of the general committee, stepped in, he made futile attempts to say the final words. More and more waves of shouts were heard: "Tuljak" was demanded. The general leaders of the song festival had doubts because it was not planned in the song list, nor was it rehearsed, but the

cries of "Tuljak, tuljak..." continued unabated. Finally, a director stepped on as the leader: A. Kasemets and under his direction, the powerful choir version of "Tuljak" enthralled the guests and surprised the leaders and singers themselves.)

(*Kool*, found in 1999 DP Kroonika)

Director Anton Kasemets showed extemporaneous cultural leadership that day, responding to the crowd and leading the choir in a rousing rendition of "Tuljak." He, Udo Kasemets, August Pruul, and Roman Toi were the chief choir directors of the Augsburg Song Festival, joining many other distinguished musicians in the DP camps who helped boost Estonian spirits through choir singing and song festivals. When the Germans retreated from Estonia and the Soviets returned, more than 70,000 Estonians fled. Among those were many key Estonian song festival leaders such as Juhan Aavik, Anton Kasemets, and Verner Nerep. Estonian choral directors, composers, and musicians arrived in the camps—without scores or instruments—and worked to build choirs, train singers, compose and arrange music, and coordinate song festivals.

Estonian refugees in DP camps included many highly trained musicians from Estonia's longstanding music community. Many Estonian musicians had studied at the Tallinn Music Conservatory, founded in 1919, where they focused on Estonian music. At the conservatory,

Figure 5.1 Augsburg Song Festival parade, chief directors from left: Roman Toi, August Pruul, Anton Kasemets, and Udo Kasemets

"their teachers were the Estonian musical luminaries of the National Awakening, composers and musicians who came of age at the early national song festivals" (Puderbaugh, 2006:33). The refugee musicians were enthusiastic about Estonian music, and they identified strongly with their culture's choral traditions. The Estonian Singers Union (ESU), founded in 1921, promoted the national song festivals, published a music journal, and helped distribute information about choral events. Most Estonian directors and composers were members of the ESU, which the Soviet Union later abolished.

Head choir director—Anton Kasemets: 1898–1978

The leader of the head conductors at the 1947 Augsburg Song Festival (Figure 5.1) was well-known Estonian director Anton Kasemets, who was born December 10, 1890, in Rapla, Estonia. He studied organ and composition at Petersburg Conservatory in 1908–1914. He moved to Tallinn, Estonia, where he was the Tallinn Conservatory choir director from 1929 to 1933. Kasemets was a head choral director with Juhan Simm at the 8th Estonian Song Festival in 1923, which featured all-Estonian choral music. He was a chief choral director again at the 9th Estonian Song Festival in 1928, along with Juhan Aavik and Leenart Neumann. This festival was the first to be held in the new Song Festival Amphitheatre, which is still used today. For the 9th festival, the ESU provided training courses for choral conductors as well as rehearsals in local towns, so Kasemets traveled to many choirs and became well known in Estonian music communities.

Kasemets escaped to Germany in 1944 with his wife, Adele Leontine Kasemets (Tamberg), and their son Udo Kasemets. They settled in the Geislingen DP camp. While there, Kasemets directed the women's choir, taught music, and directed the choir at GEG (Geislingen Eesti Gümnasium, the Estonian high school in Geislingen). Kasemets' experience as a director of song festivals in Estonia made him the logical choice for Head Choral Director at the 1947 Augsburg Song Festival. He was also on the planning committee and prepared the materials for the program that was printed in Geislingen for the Augsburg song festival. He immigrated with his wife to Detroit, Michigan, USA, where he was active in the Estonian community. He served as the Chairman of the Estonian Evangelical Lutheran Church of Michigan from 1950 (the year the congregation was formed) until 1953. He was the organist in the church there from 1950 until he moved to Canada in 1963. He died January 11, 1978, in Toronto, Ontario.

Udo Kasemets: 1919–2014

One of the head conductors in the 1947 Augsburg Song Festival was Udo Kasemets, son of director Anton Kasemets. Udo was born November 16, 1919, in Tallinn, Estonia. Before WWII, he studied piano and composition at the Tallinn Music Conservatory where he was particularly influenced by the composer Heino Eller. The younger Kasemets directed the Tallinn mixed choir, Lauluhöim, from 1941 until he left Estonia in 1944. He escaped to Germany with his parents, where he studied music in Stuttgart and Damstadt. He directed the mixed choir in Geislingen, which participated in the 1947 Augsburg Song Festival. His choral composition *Oi sünnimaa* (Oh, birthland) was performed by the mixed choir at the 1947 Augsburg Song Festival.

After WWII, Kasemets studied at the Staatliche Hochschule in Stuttgart and the Kranichstein Institut in Darmstadt, graduating with a degree in composition in 1951. He emigrated to Canada that year and continued his work as composer, teacher, and conductor. He taught piano, theory, compositions, and conducting at the Hamilton Conservatory of Music and conducted the Hamilton Conservatory Chorus. He was music critic for the *Toronto Daily Star* and taught at the Brodie School of Music and Modern Dance.

Kasemets' early works contained many settings of Estonian folk tunes: 1954s "String Trio, metamorphoses on an Estonian folk tune" is one such work. He also used indigenous Canadian folk music, for example in "Recitative and Rondo for Strings on Copper Eskimos" (1954). He became known as a leading Canadian composer and was particularly influenced by John Cage and experimentalism. One indication that his early work in the DP camps may have influenced his composition is his emphasis on survival. It has been noted that he was greatly motivated to use composition to bring

> into stark relief the very question of survival. Hence there was a certain urgency in Kasemets' creative activities to open up the Western psyche to the immensity of the changes taking place by introducing us to alternative ways of thinking and perceiving through artistic creation.
>
> (http://www.thecanadianencyclopedia.com/articles/emc/udo-kasemets)

In 1978 Kasemets organized the first Toronto Festival of Music and Technology. An avid music festival director from his early life in

Estonia and Germany, he helped develop many contemporary music festivals in Canada. Kasemets was an associate of the Canadian Music Centre and a member of the Canadian League of Composers. Kasemets died January 19, 2014, at the age of 94 in Toronto, Ontario.

August Pruul: 1907–1984

August Pruul directed the combined women's choirs at the 1947 Augsburg Song Festival as well as some of the combined choir songs at the end of the festival. He marched in the parade as a head conductor while the 50 members of his Hanau mixed choir marched not far behind. Pruul was born in 1907 in Virumaa, Estonia. He studied music at Tallinn Music Conservatory, graduating in 1931. He was the Viljandi Gümnasium music teacher and Viljandi church organist from 1941 to 1944. He escaped in 1944 to the Hanau, Germany DP camp with his wife and young children, Vaike (born 1939) and Hendrik (born 1942), along with his violin. In the Hanau DP camp, Pruul directed the Estonian mixed choir and was the UNRRA children's school music teacher. His wife, Meta-Rosalie Pruul (1912–1981), was a coloratura soprano and choir conductor who also organized choirs in the camps and sang solos. Their time in the DP camp is remembered by their daughter Vaike Pruul, even though she was very young; when the war ended, the Pruuls were in the American zone, and so

> the advent of the Americans heralded a time of renewed musical activity for our parents. Hitherto they had been organizing concerts and conducting choirs in the camp. Both Mama and Papa were conductors and with Mama also being a singer, they were very involved with singing and choirs. There were quite a few children in the camp, and they formed several children's choirs.
>
> (Pruul, V. email correspondence, August 30, 2013)

The Pruul family immigrated to Adelaide, Australia. Once there, August Pruul directed the Adelaide Estonian mixed choir and his wife, Meta, directed the Adelaide Estonian Ladies Choir "Ilo." Both August and Meta Pruul were frequent vocal soloists in Adelaide and at the Australian Estonian Days. Pruul died in Gawler, Australia, on October 9, 1984.

Dr. Roman Toi: 1916–2018

Roman Toi was the last living head conductor from the 1947 Augsburg festival. He was a gracious and humble gentleman who granted me interviews several times. Toi was the director for the men's choirs at festival as well as one of the conductors for the mixed choir numbers. Toi was born in Suure-Jaani, Viljandimaa Estonia on June 18, 1916. He studied the organ, composition, and choral conducting at Tallinn Music Conservatory and then conducting at the Mozarteum University in Salzburg. He returned to Tallinn and was working in an Estonian radio station in October 1944 when Russian (Soviet) troops moved back into Estonia. He photographed the many Estonian scores in the radio library and took the film negatives with him to ensure that, with his escape, those compositions would survive. He found his way to Germany with his wife, Vaiki Toi (1918–2002), and two-year-old son, Ants. They went to Altenstadt and then Geislingen, Germany, where he worked on a Bavarian farm and continued to compose choral music, play the organ, and direct choirs. Having established and directed the 120-voice Geislingen Estonian Men's Choir, Toi wrote "Pea Vastu" and "Karmis Ajas" for the men's choir. Two years after emigrating to Montreal, Canada, in 1949 he moved to Toronto and became a Canadian citizen in 1957. Toi conducted the Toronto Estonian mixed choir from 1957 to 1972.

He received his Doctor of Philosophy in Composition from Union Graduate School, Ohio, in 1977 with a PhD dissertation about "Estonian Folk Music." In 1976 he founded Estonia Choir (85 voices) and toured internationally, including taking trips to Estonia in 1989 and 1990. He has conducted at countless song festivals in Canada, the USA, Europe, and Australia. In addition to many instrumental works, he composed over 80 choral works. His Estonian choral music, such as "Järv leegib" (West Coast Estonian Days 1973) and "Suur on Jumal" (West Coast Estonian Days 1995), is often featured at choral festivals. He wrote extensively for men's choirs. The New York Estonian Male Chorus included three of Toi's compositions on their 1964 recording—"Kui Tume" (How Gloomy), "Kanneldaja" (The Kannel Player), and "Meri" (The Sea). Roman Toi was one of the honorary conductors at the 1990 Estonian Song Festival in Tallinn, where his composition based on an Estonian folk song, "Aiut taiut" (Waking Up), was performed by the mixed choir.

Toi was the featured conductor at Estonia's return to freedom in the 1994 Song Festival in Tallinn, Estonia. He traveled to Tallinn again in 2014 for the XXVI Song Festival as the guest of honor at the age of 98. Dr. Roman Toi contributed tremendously to the resilience of Estonian culture and the unity of the world through choral music in the amazing 101 years of his musical life.

Other choir directors in the DP camps

The following information regarding choirs that performed at the song festival in Germany 1947 is listed by Kool in DP Kroonika: Eesti pagulased Saksamaal 1944–1951. Many directors besides the chief festival directors are included. The attending choirs were primarily choirs from the American Zone, apart from the Lüübecki Eest Segakoor, which was from Lübeck in the British Zone. Some information is available about these and other DP camp choir directors is available, though for some there is scant known beyond their names.

Choir	*Director*
Ansbach segakoor (Ansbach mixed choir)	H. Jaanson
Augsburg Naiskoor (Augsburg women's choir)	Marta Kaasik
Augsburg segakoor (Augsburg mixed choir)	Meta Noorkukk
Blomberg segakoor (Blomberg mixed choir)	A. Neiländer
Eesti Insenerkompanii Meeskoor (Estonian engineer co. men's choir)	Rein Neggo
Geislingen meeskoor (Geislingen men's choir)	Roman Toi
Geislingen segakoor (Geislingen mixed choir)	Udo Kasemets
Geislingen naiskoor (Geislingen women's choir)	Anton Kasemets
Hanau segakoor (Hanau mixed choir)	August Pruul
Ingolstad meeskoor (Ingolstad men's choir)	J. Arike
8090 Lab. Serv. Co meeskoor (8090 laboratory service men's choir)	E. Sepa
Kempten sega (Kempten mixed choir)	Albert Pruks
Aschaffenburg sega (Aschaffenburg mixed choir)	Elmar Aru
Lübek sega (Lübek mixed choir)	August Ruut
Memmingen meeskoor (Memingen mixed choir)	E. Pohl
Valga laagri naiskoor (Valga camp women's choir)	Benita Tamm
Weilandshagen segakoor (Weilandshagen mixed choir)	M Suursööt
Virkhaus segakoor (Virhaus mixed choir)	Adalbert Virkhaus

Marta Kaasik: 1893–1974

Marta Kaasik was born in Valga, Estonia in 1893. She studied the piano and voice at the Tallinn Music Conservatory and graduated in 1926. She was a piano and music teacher at the Tõrva Reaalgümnaasium from 1926 to 1937 and at the Tartu Pedagoogium with Miina Härma, 1937–1944. In 1944 she fled to Augsburg, Germany, where she directed the women's choir and taught music in the Augsburg Estonian Secondary School. She directed the Augsburg women's choir and was the local choir coordinator for the Augsburg Song Festival in

1947. She emigrated in 1949 to Seabrook, NJ, where she directed the Seabrook Women's Choir. She died on October 17, 1974.

Hans Lepsa

A graduate of the Riga Conservatory, Hans Lepsa was the mixed choir director in Augsburg. He had been a chairman for the Estonian Song Festival committee in Estonia during the freedom years.

Aino Mägi: 1909–2007

Aino Onno Mägi was born in March 1909 in Võru, Estonia. Her father was a farmer who played the organ and violin. He also taught the children to sing chorales and harmonize together. She was always singing, mentioning, "Music was popping so much out of my body everything I did I was singing. When I left my house I started to sing and while I cut wood and when I came home" (1991). She said her father told them that music was "an education I can give you. Nobody can ever take this from you. It's worth more than material or wealth" (1991). In the local Estonian elementary school she learned violin and singing, but her biggest influence was family:

> The whole Onno clan was very musical Great-Grandfather Hindrik Onno, a lay preacher, was the first to own an organ in the area. He built it. My voice had grown into a soprano and Salme's alto. She was very skillful at creating alto parts to songs thus we could sing in duet any song. We sang everywhere and even performed on the Kannel Society stage. Konts was a good tenor, and Volli, an exceptional bass. We sang in the Kannel Society mixed choir. When the four of us arrived at the practice, the director would say that now we can start the Onnos are here.
>
> (1996:18)

Aino went to the Seminar for Teachers school, where she took piano lessons and was the choir's lead soprano. In 1934, she married Tarmo Mägi and moved to Saaremaa Island, where she was a teacher and church choir director.

The political climate became dangerous for anyone involved in public life around the advent of WWII. The Mägis moved from Saaremaa to Parnu in 1941 during the German occupation. Germans had occupied their area during WWII, so when the Russians reentered Estonia in 1944, they knew they would need to leave. Aino's husband was not home, but she knew she had to leave quickly with their two young children. They planned to go to Sweden, but the boat never showed up. She found a German officer who gave her a permission note to get on a German boat, and she headed out to sea with her two children and sister. They were transferred many times, as the policy was to try to consolidate ethnic groups in particular camps. Later, her family was moved to Stolzenburg, to Greven, to Oltenburg, and finally to Lingen. "Each camp contained different people from the last one, and the choir had to be started anew" (Mägi, 1991).

The family tried to get permission to go to Canada, Australia, and England, but none of them wanted a doctor and a teacher. In January 1950 they finally secured permission to go to a farm in Virginia if they agreed to work as laborers there for two years. When they finished their time on the farm they moved to New Jersey, close to New York. At that time there were 8,000 Estonians in New York and it became a cultural hub for Estonians in the United States. Mägi directed the local Girl Scout Choir, joined the New York Estonian Women's Choir—directed by Meta Noorkukk—and performed as a soloist at Estonian events. In 1957, Aino Mägi moved to Seattle where there was also a thriving Estonian community. Mägi formed the Seattle Estonian Choir and directed it until 1991. She was the music coordinator, singer, and choir director for many *Lääneranniku Eesti Päevad* (West Coast Estonian Days) festivals, including the 1981 and 1991 festivals in Seattle. She died September 19, 2007, and is remembered as a beloved leader in the Seattle Estonian music community.

Meeme Mälgi: 1902–1976

Violin-maker Meeme Mälgi was born in Tartu, Estonia. He studied at the Tartu Teacher School and learned to make violins. He escaped after WWII to Germany and was in the Geislingen DP camp, where he was head of the Geislingen Estonian Gümnasium. He directed choirs there and helped coordinate song festivals. He continued making violins, many of which are owned by Estonians, including Estonian-American Taavo Virkhaus, in the US and Canada today. He emigrated to New York in 1949, where he continued to make violins until his death in 1976.

Rein (Reinhold) Neggo: 1918–2007

Rein Neggo was born May 13, 1918 in Saaremaa, Estonia. After graduating from Saaremaa Secondary School in 1937, he studied at the City of Tartu University Faculty of Theology and studied music at the Tartu Music School. In 1944 he fled to Germany and lived in DP camps in Murnau and Geislingen. He directed the 45-member Eesti Insenerkompanii Meeskoor (Estonian Engineering Company Men's Choir) in Frankfurt, which performed at the Augsburg Song Festival in 1947 and is pictured in the 1948 photo of the Estonian Men's Choir in Geislingen. He emigrated to the USA in 1949 and worked as machinist, draftsman, and teacher in Los Angeles. He started the Los Angeles Estonian mixed choir in 1949 and organized the Estonian Lutheran Church there. As there was no Estonian minister available, he studied and was ordained as a Lutheran minister to provide services in Estonian. He brother Johannes Neggo was the organist for the congregation. He turned the choir over to Jaak Kukk (1925–2016) in 1991. Kukk directed it until 2003 when he turned the baton over to Kaie Pallo.

Meta Noorkukk: 1912–1993

Meta Noorkukk was born in Kodavere, Estonia. She studied organ and choir conducting at Tallinn Conservatory and worked as an organist in Narva and Tallinn. She started the mixed choir in 1945 in Hochfeld, turning the directing of that group over to R. Andressoo, who later turned it over to Hans Lepsa. Noorkukk formed the Augsburg Women's Choir through the YMCA. This group was later directed by Marta Kaasik and performed at the Augsburg Song Festival in 1947. Noorkukk was also the organist for the Estonian congregation in Augsburg and performed many solo concerts there. She emigrated to New York, where she was the New York Estonian Women's Choir director from 1950 to 1955.

Adalbert Virkhaus: 1880–1960

Adalbert Virkhaus was born in Väägvere, Estonia, in 1880. He graduated in 1908 from the Conservatory of Leipzig. He worked from 1909 to 1912 in theater and from 1918 to 1943 in Tartu as a music teacher and conductor. He was considered the founder of Estonian brass music.

One of Virkhaus's former students saw his name on the June 1941 list of people to be deported to Siberia by the Russians and tipped him off. The family left for Tartu in two hours and narrowly avoided being deported. They left August 22, 1944 from Tallinn on a German ship to Gotenhafen (Virkhaus, 2008). He tried to get a job in Danzig, but there were 1.2 million refugees there by then and no jobs. They went to a refugee camp in Sudenteul, where he worked as a translator since he spoke both Russian and Estonian. When the war ended, he received a safe conduct pass to Pilsen in the American Zone and then to Geislingen, where he directed the Virkhaus Segakoor. He came to the United States in 1949. His son Taavo Virkhaus, born June 29, 1934, learned violin in the DP camps. In the United States, Taavo became an orchestra director and directed numerous song festivals in America as well as six in Estonia.

Scores

As the Russians moved into Estonia, most Estonians left their homes very quickly, carrying little or nothing with them. Those who left on German boats were allowed one suitcase each, often containing such necessities as diapers and food for children (Mägi interview, 1995) or handmade Estonian folk costumes (Shuey interview, 1991). Roman Toi's suitcase full of photographed scores on film was an exception to this (Toi interview, 1996).

Estonian choral music is primarily composed SATB music using sheet music. Estonians had been reading music notation and owned choral scores from song festivals in Estonia. When choirs first formed in DP camps, little to no sheet music was available. Aino Mägi helped her choir make do:

> We had no sheet music. First, I chose songs everybody knew. My sister was a good alto and she taught alto to half the group. So we started performing. ... Now we needed music. We decided with Mr. Ottan [former Tartu University Choir director] to write the music for mixed choir from memory. I wrote the soprano and alto, and he wrote the tenor and bass. My brother was also in this camp. He was very artistic, wrote beautiful calligraphy, and volunteered to write the songs down for the choir and bind the music into notebooks. Alas, we did not have paper. But the soldiers found us paper. My brother Volli was very artistic: he wrote songs down on those letter-papers in calligraphy with decorations and bound them in a neat book. The cover was of brown paper with beautiful decoration. Much later here in USA, I compared this music with [the] originals and found how unbelievably few errors we [had] made. My notebook had a brown cover of heavier paper illustrated with a nostalgic picture of a farm. [This particular notebook is now at the Tartu Eesti Rahva Muuseum.] Later

> we got connections with other camps and copied their music for our choir. Director Adalbert Virkhaus came to Alt Garge so they copied some music that he had along. Every time someone came to camp with some music, they hand copied it. Even whole operas were hand copied.
>
> (Mägi interview, 1991)

Even writing out the scores by hand was problematic, as paper of any kind was extremely scarce. Inno Salasoo provided some examples of the sheet music used in Geislingen, noting that it was "duplicated by different methods and hand-written (not 'composed') by different persons. Also note," he said, "the different kinds of paper used—there was not much choice at the time; one had to use whatever happened to be available. Still, the choirs and the conductors did a good job" (Salasoo letter, July 1995).

Türnpu's choral piece for mixed choir "Priiuse hommikul" (Free morning) was hand-copied with very neat notation and was mimeographed in Augsburg. Since the Estonians were housed in the old Luftwaffe building, the paper the Estonians found was old order forms from the Nazi air force (Figure 5.2 and 5.3). The back side of the last two staves were preprinted letter paper in German:

> Bauleitung der Luftwaffe
> Landau a.d. Infar   Landau a.b. Infar   den_______19
> Uz________________
> NR. ___________________
> Bitte in der antwort vortehn-
> Des Gescharezeichen, das Datum
> Und furzen Inhalt anzugebe.
> Bezug:
> Betrifft:

English translation of the words on the letter paper:

> Building instructions of the air force
> Landau on the Isar file _____________ 19
> Number ______________
> Whenever you answer this request refer to the file and number
> In reference to
> Reference:
> Subject:

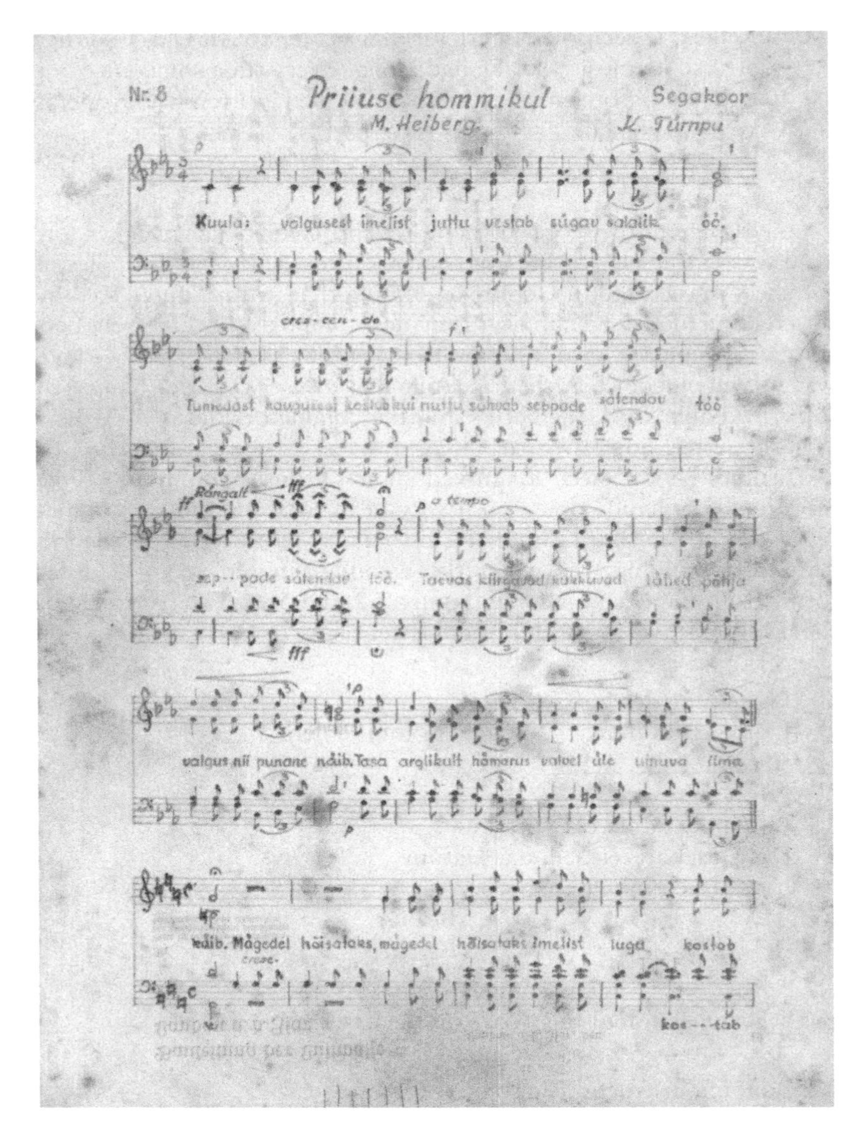

Figure 5.2 "Priiuse hommikul" by K, Türnpu handwritten score mimeographed on paper that was an old form from Nazi air force "Bauleitung der Luftvaffe, Laundau a.d. Zfar" (Building instructions of the air force) (I. Salasoo collection). Front page

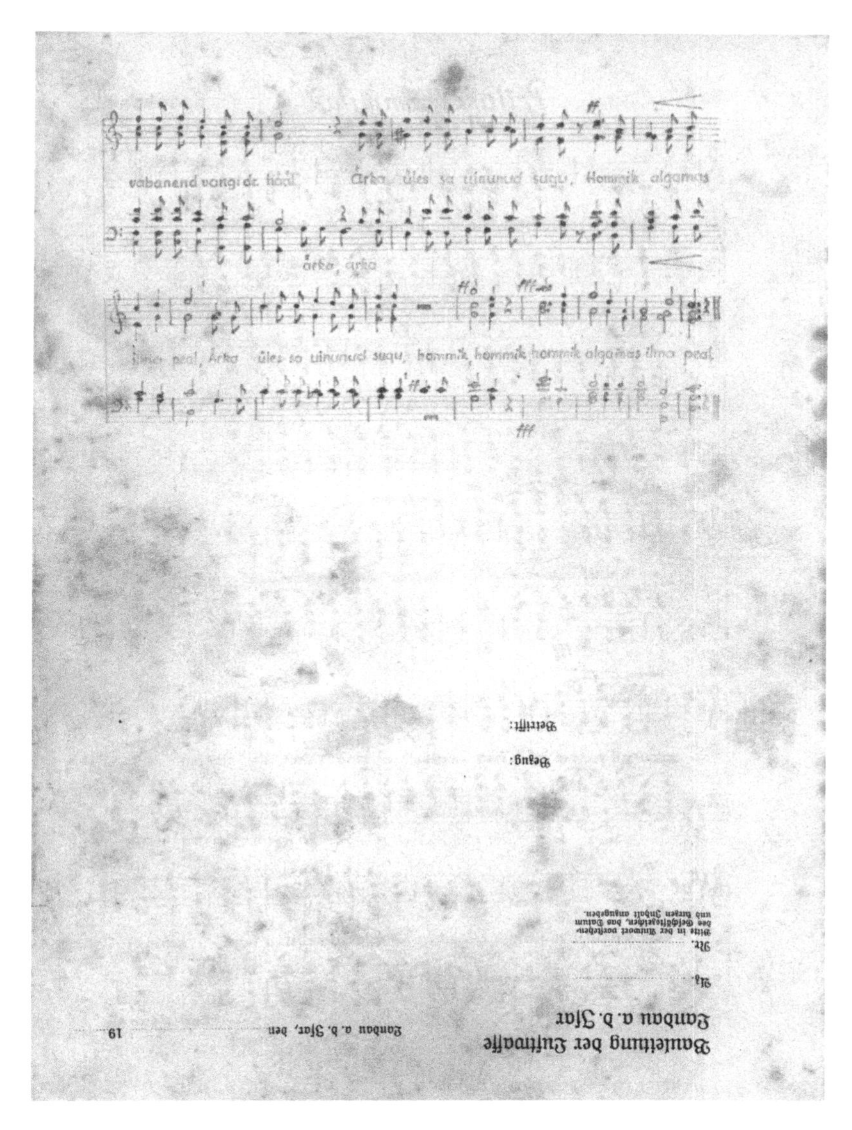

Figure 5.3 "Priiuse hommikul" by K, Türnpu handwritten score mimeographed on paper that was an old form from Nazi air force "Bauleitung der Luftvaffe, Laundau a.d. Zfar" (Building instructions of the air force) (I. Salasoo collection). Back page

Figure 5.4 "Eesti Lipp" (Estonian Flag) by E. Võru, transcribed by Albert Pruks (I. Salasoo collection)

The many choir members remembered a variety of repertoire between them, so numerous songs were added as Estonians came together in camps. Salasoo archived information about the transcribers and wrote in a letter when he sent the scores: "The music in blue, written with a very shaky hand and marked, e.g., 'Kempten, 25.IX.45.A.P.' was written by Albert Pruks, who died of cancer in Geislingen in 1948. Another song in blue (Hakkame, mehed, minema) was written by L. Mankin" (letter from Salasoo, July 1995). (Figure 5.4)

Choirs began to compile entire songbooks, several of which were published through Eugen Moegle, Buchdruckerei in Geislingen. *Vaimulikud Segakoorid* and *Vaimulikud II* and *III* were published in 1946, 1946, and 1947, respectively. *Valimik Segakoori Laule I* (Various mixed choir songs I), edited by Enn Saluveer, was printed in 1946, though no location is listed (Figure 5.5).

Repertoire of Estonian choirs in the camps

Repertoire selection in DP camps, to some degree, depended on the availability of scores. With limited supplies, the choir repertoire had to begin with music that its members knew from memory. Many of the directors and composers knew the full scores of traditional Estonian choral works well enough to write them out by hand. Most choir members in the DP camps had participated in song festivals in Estonia during the freedom years (1917–1940). At that time, they would have memorized many of the national songs since the song festivals featured all-Estonian repertoires during the years of freedom. With so many Estonian composers in the DP camps, new choral music was composed or arranged specifically for use in the Estonian choirs there. Given the churches in the camps—primarily Lutheran and some Estonian Orthodox—some sacred choral music was also part of the repertoire.

Most of the Estonian choirs were SATB, *Segakoor* (mixed choirs). Some camps also had *Naiskoor* (women's choir) and *Meeskoor* (men's choir) and in the schools there were often children's choirs. The repertoire for all of these groups was similar in that it included "Tuljak," Estonian national songs, folk song and folk tale arrangements, traditional Estonian choral music, and newly composed songs.

The first song performed in most Estonian DP camp choirs was "Tuljak." This Estonian choral classic was first performed at the 1934 song festival with the national dance, also known by the same name. When choral groups formed, this was the song all choir members would have most likely known from memory. Aino Mägi noted that they also wrote it out for newcomers, with borrowed "letter paper" from the soldiers (Mägi interview, 1995).

The tune of "Tuljak," written by Estonian choral composer Miina Härma, is a fast polka, typically sung either a cappella or with a folk

Figure 5.5 Valimik Eesti Laule III cover

music ensemble of traditional instruments such as the accordion, violin, and *kannel* (Estonian zither). The close homophonic harmony alternates with sections of sixteenth notes using tongue-twisting text while the other parts sing "hõissa ja tra la la" (hurrah and tra la la).

This difficult text is still sung at most major Estonian song festivals around the world and is considered a rite of passage for anyone learning Estonian choral music.

The lyrics by Karl Ferdinand Karlson tell the story of a wedding between Manni and Tõnni. The dance follows the story line, with partners beginning by flirting and teasing. The bridge section, where basses sing the melody line, features a swinging beat and the dancers mimic playing in a swing as they become more romantically involved. The song ends with a ritardando as the full choir sings "laskem elada" (long live all) and the female dancers are lifted in the air by the male dancers.

Tuljak text by Karl Ferdinand Karlson (1875–1941), translation:
The entire village was called together
The whole parish was invited
Guests of all sorts
Even the mayor and spouse were invited.
Tõnni, a quite eligible bachelor proposed marriage to little Manni.

A wedding, yes, a wedding,
Fifty barrels of beverages,
Food for a wedding feast,
Brought together in heaps.

Ducks and geese were roasted, fried,
More than a thousand, most likely.
A whole armory of rifles, guns,
Honor the wedding by making noise.

Is there perhaps a moon gleaming?
Do I see star or sunshine beaming?
Look at Tõnni and Manni
They walk together, hand in hand

While young Manni frolics jokingly,
The groom Tõnni laughs joyfully, tears of happiness on his face
Their world is shining brightly!
Oh, may they walk like that all their lives.

Oh brother, start playing a Viru waltz,
We wish to begin dancing.
Play and ring those Tuljak notes
That makes our blood tingle and dance.

Music kindles our hearts, dance whirls our hearts,
Guys invite you and Mom wants you to join the dance.
But why does my heart jump, quiver and shake
When a brave man takes me in his arms?

Don't feel bashful, little maiden, or shy.
We could woo and soon marry.
A fine horse neighs in the stable.
A gorgeous sleigh waits, to take my darling to her grand home.

What do you want, Tõnni's father?
The dancing is fine and the music merry, so let's go dancing,
Hurrah!
Tõnni's father asks Manni's mother to join the dance.
Let's cheer. Long live the old man and old woman!

National music was particularly important at the Augsburg Song Festival, as Estonians sought to maintain their culture in the diaspora while knowing that their songs were being suppressed by the Soviets at home. Musicologist Göran Folkestad has noted that the "impact of national music, including national anthems, as a symbol for national identity seems to be especially strong in countries in which people were not allowed to express their nationality in public for certain periods of time" (2002:155). This was clearly true for the Estonians, who often had to repress their national identity. Since around 1860 with the "Time of Awakening" (*Ärkamise Aeg*), when Estonia was breaking free of tsarist Russia, Estonian choral composers have produced a large body of national songs. Since these were composed primarily to be sung at the large, outdoor song festivals, the "archetypal festival song was predominantly homo-rhythmic, a texture necessitated by the choir's size, numbering in the tens of thousands, and the acoustical dilemma the open-air performance posed" (Puderbaugh, 2006:44).

Traditionally Estonian choral music was steeped in German hymnal styles. However, as Estonians began to further their own musical study, most attended the St. Petersburg conservatory at first, and later the Tallinn Conservatory. There was also a growing desire for a separate Estonian choral style. Olt notes that at the 7th song festival in 1910

> tradition based on the German liedertafel repertory collided with the intentions of composers like Rudolf Tobias, Artur Kapp and

> Mart Saar. Choral singing, fulfilling a vital function in satisfying man's need for self-expression and as a manifestation of people's national feelings, had grown into a powerful element of culture. On folk music and various foreign models, a national choral style had evolved with folk accents and elements having a definite place. (1980:28)

Estonian composers made it a patriotic goal to write music in an Estonian style and to use characteristic Estonian elements in their compositions. These newer, more characteristically Estonian choral pieces were particularly important at the Augsburg Song Festival.

The Estonian national song style makes effective use of Estonian vowels and emphasizes singing in harmony. An excellent example is "Koit" (Dawn) by Mihkel Lüdig. This song was first performed at the 1923 song festival in Tallinn and since 1969 has been the opening song for Estonian song festivals in Estonia and in the diaspora. Most national songs are focused on bold chords built with vocal parts moving together or paired, such as in the opening bars of "Koit." They often include passages with voices alternating men (tenor and bass) and women (soprano and alto) ("Koit," bars 5 & 6 or 8 & 9). Dotted rhythms are frequently used (see "Koit," bars 6–10), and bold octaves are featured. The opening of another national song, *Kostke laulud* (Songs Be Heard) by Martin Lipp, for instance, features the choir singing "in octaves, reinforcing the significance of the statement. A martial air pervades the work, created by dramatic dotted-eighth/sixteenth figures in the key of G minor" (Puderbaugh, 2008:34)

Estonian language has consistent emphasis on the first syllable of each word. The impact on rhythm is that there will often be frequent metric changes to coordinate with the text. In general, the rhythms are more intricate than in a hymn tune, for instance. There are frequent eighth note triplets and quarter note triplets interspersed within a duple meter. The text drives the rhythm so there are often different rhythms in multiple verses. However, in national songs, these do not get overly esoteric or complex, so they can be performed by the large groups at song festivals.

The Estonian language is particularly beautiful for choral text because it is vowel rich. There are nine vowels in Estonian that are used for more than half of the sounds. The vowels can be simple, long, or over-long, making choral music ring when sung with pure pronunciation. One of the most famous national Estonian poets wrote the text for *Mu isamaa on minu arm*, a poem that has been used for multiple national songs.

Mu isamaa on minu arm text by Lydia Koidula (1843–1886)

Mu isamaa on minu arm,
kel südant annud ma.
Sull' laulan ma, mu ülem õnn,
mu õitsev Eestimaa!
Su valu südames mul keeb,
su õnn ja rõõm mind rõõmsaks teeb,
mu isamaa, mu isamaa!

Mu isamaa on minu arm,
ei teda jäta ma,
ja peaksin sada surma ma
see pärast surema!
Kas laimab võõra kadedus,
sa siiski elad südames,
mu isamaa, mu isamaa!

Mu isamaa on minu arm,
ja tahan puhata,
su rüppe heidan unele,
mu püha Eestimaa!
Su linnud und mull' laulavad,
mu põrmust lilled õitsetad,
mu isamaa, mu isamaa!

My fatherland is my love,
My fatherland is my love
to whom I have given my heart,
I sing to you, my supreme fortune,
my blooming Estonia!
Your pain boils in my heart,
your fortune and joy make me glad,
my fatherland, my fatherland!

My fatherland is my love,
I will never leave him,
and should I die a hundred deaths
because of it!
If foreign envy is slandering,
you still live in my heart,
my fatherland, my fatherland!

My fatherland is my love,
and I want to rest,
I lay into your arms,
my sacred Estonia!
Your birds will sing me to sleep,
you will bloom flowers from my ashes,
my fatherland, my fatherland!

Another important poet, Estonian pastor Martin Lipp (1854–1923), wrote the text for *Kostke laulud* (Touch the songs) during the "Time of Awakening." The text uses many national themes, including aspects of Estonian folklore, references to iconic folk instruments like the kannel, reverence for the Estonian language, and folk figures such as Vanemuine and Kalevala:

Kostke laulud (Songs Be Heard)

Songs be heard in Estonian
And accompanied by kannel
In Estonian language with Estonian soul
Let's unite the homeland
One mind, one language
With the power of Vanemuine
Let the songs be heard in Estonian
Accompanied by kannel
The spirit of Estonia has resisted
Plague and famine times
Estonian men have brought swords
And defeated the enemies
We have courage
We have always had courage
Let's sing in Estonian
Accompanied by kannel

There are many beloved national poems that have been used across multiple choral compositions. While in the Geislingen DP camp in 1947, Udo Kasemets used a poem called "Ta Lendab Mesipuu Poole" (He flies toward the beehive) by Juhan Liiv (1864–1913) for a mixed choral composition. The same poem was used by Peep Sarapik (1943–1994) for the choral song now featured as a national song in most Estonian song festivals.

Many Estonian choral works are based on traditional Estonian folk songs and folk tales. Sometimes an actual regilaul (old song) is used in an arrangement, as is the case with "Laulik" (Singer) by Evald Aav, which was sung at a Greven choral concert in 1949. This arrangement is based the text of the common opening regilaul song "Kui mina hakken laulemaie" (When I start singing). Anton Kasemets composed "Minu Tõnn" (My Tõnn) based on the folksong about Tõnn and Mann, two common names also used for the lovers in the song "Tuljak." Kasemets' composition is a waltz-like song that is "elavalt ja kargelt" (lively and crisp). It begins with a verse about Tõnn sung by the sopranos and altos, then a verse about Mann sung by the tenors and basses followed by a boisterous ending with the women singing a final chord on "Tõnn" while the men sing the chord on "Mann." This arrangement of the folksong was published in the *Segakoorid III*, which was printed in 1947 by EKK in Geislingen. There are many arrangements of this popular folksong, including a women's choir version by Võrk that was sung by the combined women's choirs at the 1947 Augsburg festival.

Another folk song arrangement in the *Segakoorid III* is "Naabri Mari" (Neighbor Mari) by Udo Kasemets, which more closely follows the regilaul format with repeated text on the first half of three verses and an echo section on each of the three verses. It follows the Estonian text rhythmically and is listed as "lõbusalt" (with fun/cheer).

Some songs featured traditional folk tale heroes such as Kalev, from the Estonian epic poem *Kalevipoeg* (much like the Finnish Kalev epic). In fact, the opening mixed choir song at the 1947 Augsburg festival was "Veel kaitse, kange Kalev" (Still protect, mighty Kalev). The text by Karlson talks about the hero Kalevipoeg, his mother Linda, and the Estonian folk spirit. Miina Härma composed the music for this piece, which is used at many festivals. *Kalevipoeg* characters are featured in many compositions used in the camps, such as "Troost (Kalevipoeg)" by K. Türnpuu, printed in the Geislingen *Valimik Segakoori Laule I* (Free Estonian mixed choir songs I) (1946).

The 1947 Augsburg Song Festival program included several pieces that were newly composed by directors and composers in the DP camps. Director Udo Kasemets wrote the words and music for "Oi, sünnimaa" (Oh, birthplace). His father, director Anton Kasemets, composed the music for "Ju kumab koit" (Glowing dawn). Choir director Roman Toi wrote "Pea Vastu" (Hang on) and director Valdeko Loigu wrote "Lõpp ja algus" (End and beginning). The camps were full of composers who enthusiastically added to the repertoire available for the choirs in the camps and later in the diaspora.

The repertoire in the DP camps included works primarily by Estonian composers. Only a few folksongs from Finnish or Latvian composers were included and those were translated into Estonian. The sacred music used in church services was primarily Estonian, though works by Beethoven or Schubert were occasionally used.

Many of the Estonian composers who featured in WWII choral concerts and festivals died before the time of the choirs in the WWII DP camps (Karl August Hermann, 1851–1909; Miina Härma, 1864–1941; Konstantin Türnpuu, 1865–1927; Rudolf Tobias, 1873–1918; Evald Aav, 1900–1939). Some Estonian composers remained in Estonia after the war, Edgar Arro, Gustav Ernesaks, Artur Kapp, Eugene Kapp, Cyrillus Kreek, Aleksander Läte, Mihkel Lüdig, Eduard Oja, Mart Saar, Tuudur Vettik, and Enn Võrk among them. These composers were expected to compose according to the rules of the Soviet committee and had varying degrees of success in Soviet-controlled Estonia.

It is estimated that about 200 Estonian musicians escaped from Soviet-controlled Estonia, including composers, instrumentalists, singers, and teachers (Aavik, 1961:12). There were composers who escaped to Sweden (Juhan Aavik, P. Ardna, and H. Olt) and Germany (Albert Pruks, Anton Kasemets, Roman Toi, Valdeko Loigu, and Udo Kasemets) and carried on composing Estonian choral music as part of the diaspora.

Among the thousands of important Estonian choral composers, the few names of those featured in DP choir concerts and song festivals that are collected here give an idea of the type of composers featured in WWII choral events. Composers who were also notable conductors are covered in addition to those mentioned earlier in this chapter.

Evald Aav (1900–1939) received his degree in composition from Tallinn conservatory in 1926. He composed the first Estonian opera, *Vikerlased (The Vikings)*. He studied composition with Artur Kapp and music theory with Anton Kasemets, who served as one of the Augsburg song festival conductors in the DP camps. Aav was a popular choral composer in Estonia and the general conductor of the 1938 Song festival (XI Laulupidu). Aav's choral composition *Murelaul* (Song of Concern) was performed in Oldenburg in 1949 and *Laulik* (The Singer) in Greven in 1949. *Laulik* uses "*kui mina hakkan laulemaie*" (When I begin to sing), a common regilaul text, in a folkloric choral arrangement.

Juhan Aavik (1884–1982) studied at St. Petersburg conservatory and became professor and Director of the Tallinn Conservatory (1933–1944). He was the chief conductor of the Estonian Song Festivals in

Tallinn in 1928, 1933, and 1938. Aavik escaped to Sweden when the Soviets moved into Estonia after WWII. He composed over 200 choral compositions with most of his works being based on folk music. Aavik's mixed choir composition *Meie laulame* (We sing) was sung at the 1947 Augsburg Song Festival. His choral work, *Noorte laul* (Youth song) was performed at the Kempten 1948 song festival. Aavik kept in close contact with the Estonian refugees in Germany and sent greetings that were read at the 1947 Augsburg Song Festival.

Edgar Arro (1911–1978) was born in Tallinn and studied at the Tallinn Conservatory of Music. He graduated with degrees in organ and composition. He remained in Estonia after WWII and was the secretary of the Estonian SSR Union of Composers from 1952 to 1966. He taught music theory at the Tallinn Conservatory from 1972 to 1978. He wrote over 130 choral works. He was best known for his operetta *Rummu Jüri*.

Gustav Ernesaks (1908–1993) was a key figure in Estonian choral composition and Song Festival organization. He was born in Perila, Estonia and graduated from the Tallinn Conservatory in music pedagogy in 1931. He taught in the Tallinn Conservatory beginning in 1934 and directed choirs there from 1944 to 1974. He founded the National Estonian Male Choir in 1944 and composed many pieces for men's choirs. He was an important song festival organizer and helped design the new song festival grounds at Tallinn in 1960. Many of his pieces have become classic staples of the song festival repertoire, including *Hakkame, mehed minema* (Men, let's get started), which was sung from handwritten copies at the Kempten festival. Ernesak's *Noor kevede* (Young spring day) was sung by the women's choir at the Augsburg 1947 song festival. His composition *Mu Isamaa on Minu Arm* (My Native Land, My Dearest Love) has become an important anthem at song festivals. Ernesaks remained in Estonia after WWII and continued to compose, direct choirs, and organize song festivals. His works include more than 300 a cappella choral works.

Miina Härma (1864–1941), sometimes spelled Minna Herman, is the composer of the beloved dance song, *Tuljak*. Along with *Tuljak*, many of her songs were sung by choirs in the DP camps, including *Tule koju* (Come home), *Kojuigatsus* (Longing for Home), and *Veel kaitse kange Kalev* (Still Protect, Mighty Kalev), which was sung at the 1947 Augsburg Song Festival. Härma studied with Karl Hermann, then at St. Petersburg Conservatory, graduating with degrees in organ performance and composition in 1890. She was an organist and a choir director for many years. She collected folk music of Estonia and helped organize many choral festivals. She is the composer of over 200 choral works. Härma was considered a hard taskmaster who expected hard work and devotion from her choir members and students. She, herself, felt the need to completely devote herself to her work, saying:

> *Muusika on kallis kirg. Ta nõuab oma sõpradelt andumust ihu ja hinge poolest. Ta on armukade, maksab kätte ja purustab töö, kui temale täiesti ei anduta. Suur muusika ei ole ainult elusiht, vaid ta peab olema ka eluülesanne.*
>
> Music is a dear passion. It requires [the] devotion of body and soul. It is jealous, vengeful and destroys the work if the person does not completely devote to it. Great music is not only for life's goal, but also our life's mission.
>
> (1937 quote by Härma in "Muusikaleht" number 2, page 36. EestiTeatri- ja Muusikamuuseem, 2009:5)

Karl August Hermann's (1851–1909) mixed choir piece *Troostilaul* (Comforting song) was sung at the first Geislingen summer concert in 1946. Hermann was an important figure in the Time of Awakening, and was an Estonian language lecturer at University of Tartu, the editor of *Eesti Postimees*, folk song collector, promoter of Estonian music, song festival organizer, and publisher of Estonian music compilations. He composed thousands of choral songs including *Kungla Rahvas* (Kungla people), which is immensely popular at Estonian gatherings. He wrote simple and folk-like melodies that were known for their carefree and optimistic spirit.

Juhan Jürme (1896–1943) was born in Tallinn and graduated from the Tallinn Conservatory in composition and organ. His composition *Rukkirääk* (ryecakes) was performed in DP camps at Greven and Hanau. His only published collection was Kaksteist vaimulikku laulu segakooridele (Twelve Sacred Songs for Mixed Choir) published in 1927. Jürme died during WWII and most of his work disappeared at that time.

Artur Kapp (1878–1952) studied in St. Petersburg with Rimsky-Korsakov. He was a composition professor at Tallinn Conservatory and wrote organ, symphonic and large scale choral works. His choral piece *Mu süda* (My heart) was sung at the 1947 Augsburg Song Festival. He also wrote *Ei eksi* (no mistake), a frequently sung piece in the DP choirs. Kapp was one of Estonia's first composers and the composition teacher for many important composers who followed him, including Arro, Ernesaks, E Kapp, Päts, and Reiman. He remained in Estonia and retired to his hometown Suure-Jaani in 1944.

Eugene Kapp (1908–1996) was the son of composer Artur Kapp. His composition *Mets* (Forest) was part of the DP choral repertoire. Eugene Kapp was part of the State Artistic Ensembles in Yaroslavl as composer and conductor, composed patriotic Estonian and Soviet songs, and was loyal to the communistic regime, receiving many USSR awards. He was known for using folk music material in his compositions, especially in his instrumental compositions. Estonian folk music and tales were themes in his ballet music *Kalevipoeg* written in 1947.

Cyrillus Kreek (1889–1962) was born into a large musical family in west Estonia. Kreek learned the piano, trumpet, and trombone as a child. He went on to the St. Petersburg Conservatory, where he collected folk tunes and studied composition until WWI interrupted his education. Kreek taught in music schools and teachers' schools in Haapsulu, Rakvere, and Tallinn while still composing and collecting folk music. He wrote many sacred and secular choral pieces, including many arrangements of folk music and the frequently performed "Taaveti laulud" (Songs of David). His sacred choral music was often featured in DP camp church concerts. Kreek managed to continue to compose significant sacred music during the Soviet-controlled era by maintaining an aloof outward posture toward the church.

Aleksander Saebelmann Kunileid (1845–1875) conducted at the first Estonian song festival in 1869. His compositions *Mu isamaa on minu arm* (My Native Land, my Dearest Love) and *Kodu* (Home) are important national songs that were sung at the DP camp song festivals. He was a teacher at Valga Seminary and primarily arranged folk songs.

Valdeko Loigu (1911–1973) studied in the Tartu Conservatory and worked in the Vanemuine Theatre. He fled to Germany in 1944 and studied in Stuttgart. He composed and directed choirs in the Schwetzingen and Geislingen DP camps. He was the assistant conductor of the male chorus "Eesti Laulumehed" of the 8090 Lab. Service Company in the 1947 Augsburg Song Festival. He wrote *Möök varastatakse* (Stolen sword) and published a set of mixed choir compositions, "Harmoonilised koorilaulud," in 1947 in Germany ("Harmoonilised koorilaulud II," Lakewood NJ. See IHRCA box 3750). Valdeko emigrated to the United States in 1950. He conducted the Cleveland Estonian mixed choir, the New York Estonian women's choir, and the Lakewood Estonian mixed choir. Valdeko received the George Washington Honor award in the United States for his composition "Our American Home" for mixed choir and piano. He died in 1973 and his ashes were buried in Tartu, Estonia in 1997.

Aleksander Läte (1860–1948) graduated in composition from the Dresden Conservatory in 1897. He established Estonia's first symphony orchestra in 1900. His composition *Kostke laulud Eesti keeles* (Songs be heard in Estonian) was sung at the 1938 Estonian Song Festival. He was a general conductor at the fourth song festival. Läte composed *Ärka üles isamaa* as an Estonian national song, and it was one of the featured songs at the 1947 Augsburg Song Festival. During the Soviet occupation, the song was still performed in Estonia, though the interpretation of the lyrics was adapted to fit political needs (Vahter, 1963:38). Läte composed more than 200 choral works.

Mihkel Lüdig (1880–1958) studied with Rimsky-Korsakov in St. Petersburg and later at the Tallinn Conservatory. He wrote the piece that has become the traditional opening song of the festivals since the "Jubilee" (100th anniversary) Song Festival in 1969—*Koit* (Dawn). Lüdig stayed after WWII at his home in Vändra, where he received several awards from the USSR.

Jüri Mandre (1907–1970) was born in Tartu, where he studied piano. He went to the University of Tartu, though he did not complete his degree there. He worked with the Vanemuine Theatre in Tallinn until he escaped to Germany in 1944. He lived in the Augsburg DP camp, where he was the Estonian high school music teacher. He composed music there and worked with choirs and theatres in the DP camp in Augsburg. Mandre emigrated to Baltimore, Marlyand, USA in 1951 where he founded the Baltimore Estonian Men's Choir. Many of his compositions included inspiring lyrics sung in the DP camps, including *Ei kesta igavesti vägivald* (Violence will not last forever) and *Vabadus võidab* (Freedom wins) for mixed choirs. Archives of his materials can be found in the IHRCA collection, box 3129.

Eduard Oja (1905–1950) composed using elements of Estonian folk music such as *Kangakudumise laul* (weaving song), which was featured at the 1948 Kempten Song Festival. Oja studied composition with Heino Eller in Tartu and was considered a very promising young composer. Unfortunately, many of his compositions were destroyed in the fire during the bombing of the Estonia Theatre on March 9, 1944. More of his manuscripts were destroyed when a Soviet aircraft hit the Oja home in Tartu later that year. He reconstructed some of this material from memory. He died poor and withdrawn from public life in Tallinn.

Albert Eduard Pruks (1901–1949) was a musician, composer, and choral conductor in Estonia, and composed *Hällilaul* (Lullaby) in Geislingen in 1946 for his daughter Inge Pruks (Izzo).

> Family lore has it that mother did not want to leave Estonia, but that my father pressured her, saying he could not leave without her and baby Inge. Although I do not know the exact nature of

> my father's patriotic activities is seemed certain that he would be killed or sent to Siberia if he stayed. Some 60 years later, a half-sister I discovered in Estonia would tell me that our father left for other reason, too. She said he complained bitterly at hearing only Russian music on the radio and vowed to return only when Estonia was free again to express its own soul through its own music. Of course that was never to be, because my father died in the Geislingen Displaced Persons Camp in February 1949.
> (Maddisson, 2015:361)

Pruks performed, composed, and taught music while in Geislingen.

> Exile made my father feel even more keenly the power of music and he composed many songs about his longing for Estonia. Fearing perhaps that he would never see me grow up, he composed a lullaby for me in March 1946, in Geislingen, when I was only two and a half years old. It is a song which asks me not to forget Estonia.
> (Maddisson, 2015:362)

Pruks composed other choral music used in the DP camps such as *Valuguse Vaim* (Spirit of pain) and *Hallin ja kodumaa* (Hall and homeland).

Riho Päts (1899–1977) was a composer, choir conductor, and music educator in Estonia. He studied piano and composition at the Tallinn Conservatory. Päts taught music in Haapsalu (1921–1923) and many schools in Tallinn (1924–1950). In 1950 he was arrested and sent to a forced labor prison camp in Siberia. He was released in 1955 with his rights restored in 1968. From 1958 to 1971 Päts taught at the Tallinn Pedagogical University, where he employed many innovative music education practices along with the methods of Kodaly and Orff. His mixed choir compositions *Lopna Laul* (song of Lop), *Sangarite laul* (heroes song), and *Pulmalaul* (wedding song) and his men's choir composition *Jaan läeb jaanitulele* (Jaan goes to the Midsommer fire) were on many programs in the DP camps.

Mart Saar (1882–1963) was a choral composer whose works were often based on Estonian folksongs. Saar created a systematic collection of traditional Estonian folksongs in 1907 and 1910 and was the first to use regilaul melody, rhythm, harmony and performance practices in choral composition. He composed *Põhjavaim* (Spirit of the north), which was sung at the 1947 Augsburg Song Festival. His compositions *Jaan läheb jaanitulele* (Jaan goes to the midsummer fire) and *Leelo* (melody) show his fondness for folk music and helped build a national style in choral music through folk song. Saar was also a professor of composition at the Tallinn Conservatory of Music (1943–1956). Older regilaul songs fascinated Saar. He used the regilaul and their changing meters in *Läksin kõrtsi aega viitma* (I went to spend time in the tavern). Saar also used older dialect folk text in *Mis Need Ohjad Meida Hoidvad* (What are these reins holding us down?), which was sung at the 1938 festival. It "refers to the Estonian experience with feudalism before the nineteenth century" (Puderbaugh, 2008:33). Saar received the USSR Honored Worker in Arts Award in 1945 and the ESSR People's Artist Award in 1972.

Juhan Simm (1885–1959) was the chief choral conductor for the 1923 and 1933 song festivals. He was a cellist and composer. He taught at the Tartu School of Music from 1944 to1951. His mixed choir composition *Oma saar* (Our island) was featured at the Geislingen 1946 concert.

Rudolf Tobias (1873–1918) composed *Varas* (The Thief), which was sung by DP choirs in Kempten. He was an important developer of the Estonian music style and studied and taught at the St. Petersburg Conservatory. Tobias was also an organist and choir conductor for the St. Petersburg Estonian congregation at St. John's Church. Tobias is considered one of the founding Estonian composers. He used folk music material in many works, including the dramatic *Kalevipoeg*, for reciter and orchestra. He moved back to Tartu and worked there as composer, musician, and conductor from 1904 to 1908, before moving to Germany and teaching at the Royal Academy of Music in Berlin, where he died in 1918. After Estonia regained its freedom, his remains were brought back to Estonia and buried in his hometown of Kullamaa in 1992.

Konstantin Jakob Türnpuu (1865–1927) graduated from the St. Petersburg Conservatory. He worked as an organist at Niguliste Church in Tallinn and was a general conductor at song festivals V and VI. His many choral compositions include *Kevade Tunne* (Spring feeling), *Kyrie, Ei mul ole isamaja* (I have no father's home), *Lahkumise laul* (Song of Departing), *Mul lapsepölves rääkis* (I was told in childhood), *Mu armas isamaa* (my dear fatherland), and *Priiuse hommikul* (Morning), all sung in the Geislingen DP choirs. *Lahkuse laul* (Song of kindness) is about friendship and is used in the ending ceremony for West Coast Estonian Days festivals among Estonian-Americans in the United States.

Tuudur Vettik (1898–1982) was a well-known conductor of many choirs. He taught at the Tallinn Teachers' Seminar and Tallinn

Conservatory. He was the chief choral conductor of six song festivals. His many important choral compositions include a multitude sung in Augsburg, including some performed at the 1947 Song Festival, such as *Su põhjamaa päikese kullast* (your Northern sunshine of gold). Many others were sung during the DP choral events, including *Merella on sinine* (sea is blue), *Kaera Jaan* (children's song that is about Jaan), *Kas tunned maad* (Do you know the land), *Teid ma tervitan* (I salute you), and *Mu sünnimaa* (my birthland). Vettik received the ESSR Honored Worker in the Arts Award in 1947. He was imprisoned by communist authorities in 1950–1956. He was eventually allowed out and from 1956 to 1962 he again taught choral conducting at the Tallinn Conservatory. He was "rehabilitated" in 1968 (Eesti Muusika Infokeskus) and received the ESSR People's Artist Award in 1980.

Enn Võrk (1905–1962) was a composition student of Artur Kapp and graduated from the Tallinn State Conservatoire in 1926. He wrote many of the most important Estonian patriotic choral compositions, including *Eesti Lipp* (Estonian flag) *Lauljate lipulaul* (Singers' flagship), *Lilleside* (flower wrap), and *Helise ilma* (Ring clear), which were all sung at 1947 Augsburg Song Festival. In 1950, Võrk was forced to leave his Tallinn Conservatory teaching job for illegitimate reasons and his membership in the Estonian Composers' Union was taken away. He heard he might be arrested so he hid himself in the Viljandi countryside until 1955. His rights were re-established in 1959. Later, Võrk worked as a piano tuner and chief engineer in the Tallinn Piano Factory.

Estonian refugees escaped with very few material possessions, but the powerful songs of Estonian choral traditions remained accessible to them. These Estonian directors, composers, and musicians provided a memory treasure box of choral music, allowing refugees in the WWII displaced person camps to know their cultural homeland and hope for their return to a free Estonia.

6 Song festivals and resilience

Singing toward a brighter future

> Kui hingad nagu üks teistega, on su hing kohal. "When you breathe with others as one, your soul is there."
>
> (From the 2009 Estonian Song Festival program)

Estonian displaced persons (DPs) fled from Soviet-controlled Estonia with only what they could carry. They found that their return home would be far in the future, if ever. As in previous times of hardship, singing in choirs was the critical means for retaining hope, maintaining their identity, and moving forward. As one refugee remembered, "Singing did have an advantage: It was portable. Even the physically wounded of war could indulge" (Madisson, 2015:42). This culture of singing did indeed aid Estonians in the journey of healing from loss through resilience.

Loss of hope, memories, identity, and self-esteem

Extreme hardship fell on Estonians in 1939 as Russia and Germany moved in and out of their tiny country. Estonians had to decide if and when they should leave, how they should attempt to travel, what to take, who to tell, and where to go.

> The Baltic refugee's life both in the camps and previously, can be seen as a succession of interruptions. Let us look back at the nine years prior to the time under consideration, forgetting the upheavals of World War I. Since 1939 there were at least four major periods: first, life in one's own independent democratic republic; then the period under the Communist regime of 1940–1941; then three years of Nazi occupation; then flight and liberation by the Western allies; and finally, life in the DP camps. During

> the Russian and Nazi regimes especially, there were many interruptions of everyday activities; so many contradictory commandments to obey that life became a potpourri of short meaningless fragments, instead of a clear symphonic line.
>
> (Bakis, 1955:77)

This constant turmoil left many feeling hopeless. The timeline (Appendix A) shows this persistent chaotic existence for the Estonians before, during, and immediately after WWII.

Psychological upheaval exploded with the initial 1939 Soviet invasion, which crushed the new little country soon after it gained its independence from Russia in 1918. The Soviet regime, followed by the Nazi regime, took an immense emotional toll on the identity and self-esteem of Estonians. Life under such oppressive regimes is fraught with terrifying control techniques that undermine cultural identity, hope, and cohesion through propaganda, isolation, and torture. Agents came to cities, villages, and farms looking for people who did not support the new regime. People were taken from their homes for unknown reasons and were sent away or killed. The DPs were aware of the traumas that this entailed. In the explanation of conditions in Estonia, the Geislingen Estonian DP report explained that "the Red Army killed the captured Estonian soldiers and civilians, fired at refugees and drove over them with tanks, raped women and deported lots of people to Soviet Union. Terror and injustice are closely related to the Soviet System" (Estonian Displaced Persons, June 1949). The constant fear of these very oppressive regimes did indeed disrupt the emotional wellbeing of Estonians even before they decided to escape.

Oppression under foreign rule was just the start of the emotional trauma of WWII for the Estonians. Next came the difficult decisions of if, and when, to leave. Many Estonians were farmers and sailors with very strong ties to their land, their animals, their boats, and the sea. Some families had loved ones who had been conscripted into Soviet or Nazi military service, sent to Siberia, or were otherwise missing. The decision to leave was fraught with identity issues about leaving careers, family, and country. A decision often had to be made suddenly to avoid deportation, so many fled without saying goodbye to their loved ones. These lost contacts haunted many for the rest of their lives.

The journey itself was especially difficult because the war was still raging. As the escape began, the refuges were still lamenting their decision to leave and were second-guessing choices while also watching for hazards along the way. Certainly, the effect of these life-threatening times was remembered forever. The harrowing journey to escape at the end of the war is documented in many memoirs, books, and movies (i.e., Soovere, 1999; Lie et al, 2007; Hinrikus and Kirss, 2009).

Most Estonians believed they were only escaping for a short time, but that soon proved wrong. Seattle Estonian Elga Mikelson, the Augsburg Song Festival translator, shared that she left Estonia without winter clothes because she was sure they would return home by Christmas. Psychologist Eduard Bakis described this problem in his writings, elaborating on a condition he referred to as "DP apathy":

> During the first winter in the DP camps in Germany (1945–46), it seemed to the writer that the main task of a psychologist would be to find out why wartime experiences, culminating in the loss of homeland had not done more harm to these people. The morale (and maladjustments) were not as bad as had been anticipated, and the statements of visiting foreign observers—at least those made public—seemed to support this impression. Despite some minor maladjustments, humorous rather than tragic, there were neither serious complaints about misbehavior, not any feeling that something more serious would break out. The refugees believed the misery to be terminated. But time passed with no end of camp life in sight. Christmas of 1945 was believed to be the last in the camps, yet Christmas 1946 found the refugees still there and with no prospects of either returning to a liberated homeland or of emigrating.
>
> (Bakis, 1955:76).

The DPs finally realized they would not be able to go home to Estonia, making it more difficult to keep hope alive. One Estonian wrote to the American zone commander for help: "As political fugitives we cannot return to the Baltic States. For five years we have been waiting for our liberation. There are no words to describe our sufferings and misery" (IHRCA letter May 25, 1945 Gunzenhausen 2294–2358 MIC 112). The realization that return was not eminently possible did indeed take further emotional toll on the refugees.

Lingering in camp was one of the factors that depressed the DPs. Formerly active professional people felt that "the style of life reminded one of a slow-motion picture" (Bakis, 1955:77). Many DPs were found to have problems and "despite the wide variety of symptoms, ranging from violence to apathy, the most conspicuous and widespread feature seemed to be procrastination and apathy. The displaced persons named this state of disorganization 'D.P. apathy'" (Bakis, 1955:77). It was difficult for the refugees to keep hope alive under such conditions.

The shortage of calories provided produced low energy, which added to the ennui and depression. Additional problems included anger at Germany for originating the war, compressed living quarters, resentment from local German residents displaced by the DPs, worry about friends and relatives still missing, and concerns about emigrating or being sent to the Soviet Union—all of which added to the stress and loss of hope. Many were still missing family members and asked for help through the UNRRA to find them. Welfare officers would then write to the UNRRA headquarters in letters that described the problem, such as this letter housed in the IHRCA archives:

UNRRA March 11th 1946
DP Assembly Center
Kleinheubach am Main
Germany
No 256

DP Camp
Ried (InnKreis)
Kasernenstr. 10
Austria

ATTN. Welfare Officer

In our Estonian Camp lives Estonian national Mrs. Matson, Vilhelmine born 7 April, 1910 in Voru, Estonia and her three children:

Valdar born 31 January 1938
Dina born 24 July 1940
Peter born 11 May 1945
She has another two children
Boris born 29 September 1933
Kalju born 15 April 1935
Whom she lost on journey, and whom she is very anxious to find again.

As she means that some of the people living in your camp may be able to give information about the children, I ask you to make every possible investigation and let me know the result as soon as possible.

Else Wiencke
Welfare Officer

While Estonian DPs were survivors who had been through many rough times, they continued to endure great stress. This is a common theme in writing about the identity issues of all DPs.

> Exposure to inexplicable evil and cruelty can shake the foundations of the survivor's faith in the beneficence of life and humankind. The extreme violation of torture often leaves survivors with existential preoccupations in which they strive, often unsuccessfully to find a coherent reason for the abuses they have suffered. They and their communities face a crisis of trust, faith and meaning that may intensify feelings of alienation and emotional isolation.
>
> (Silove, 2005:46)

Hope and their sense of memory are easily lost amid this chaos. Life in the DP camps meant a loss of identity and control, which took a toll on morale. As time wore on in the camps, self-confidence and esteem fell to new lows, with refugees becoming severely depressed and longing for their homes and families.

The DP camps also included children who entertained different views of the situation. Seattle Estonian Taimi Moks remembers,

> For us children, life was pretty normal with going to school and playing at other times. The surrounding woods and gravel pits provided neat places. For the adults this was a terrifying and heartbreaking time. Estonia had been given to the Communists and we realized we had no hope to go back home or any other place to go.
>
> (Moks, unpub.)

Many songs, such as "Nooruse aeg" (The time of youth) at the song festivals were about children, perhaps in a bid to build on the hopefulness of youth. Youth choirs also participated in the festivals.

Promotion of emotional health and resilience was an important goal for WWII international aid organizations. Clinicians and researchers attempted to help alleviate the low morale of displaced persons, but the ardently independent Estonians felt they must take care of these morale issues themselves. Early in their cultural history, Estonians had formed a path to resilience where, in times of trouble, the song festivals were a key to renewal of spirit. The UNRRA recognized the importance of choral music for the morale of the DPs in post-WWII camps. While priority went to providing food, clothing, and shelter, the aid organizations also made major efforts to support choirs and song festivals. The immediate formation of choirs and song festivals in each of the Estonian DP camps did once again provide the Estonians with resilience through hope, memories, identity, and self-esteem. Displaced groups from Estonia's Baltic neighbors Latvia and Lithuania also found music to be a way to rebuild their sense of identity.

For Estonians, there was no question that choirs would be their salvation. But how does a choir help sustain a culture? Choirs and the song festivals in WWII DP camps did indeed provide a medium for hope and a way to hold on to memories of home. Many elements of choral singing help provide the resilience that was so needed for the Estonian refugees.

Hope and memory in a new land

Amid the horrors, memories did survive, often through song. The Estonian DPs had a vast repertoire about their homeland that helped them remember their past. As they had only recently attained independence, one might think that their musical traditions would be easily lost. However, Estonian singing traditions predated independence, with the song festivals having a history that started in 1869, long before WWII.

The foreword to the New York Estonian American songbook reminds the immigrants of the importance of memories in song, saying, "Ka eestlastele vabas maailmas on meie laul jäänud üheks kaunimaks aardeks, elustades mälestusi ning olles vaimseks sidemeks oma rahvaga." (Even in the free world of Estonians, our song has become one of the most beautiful treasures, reviving memories and being a spiritual bond with our people) (Valik Ühislaule [A Selection of Songs] "Saateks Teisele Trükile" [Guide to the Second Edition] 1948?). Remembering and being remembered is an important theme in Estonian songs. Juhan Aavik's "Meie laulame" (We sing) was sung at the 1947 Augsburg Song Festival. The lyrics by Kaljo Lepik end the song with the words "Ei iial, ei iialgi kao" (we will never disappear).

Ernst Ein, the USA-zone Estonian committee chair, wrote to the Geislingen choir on their third anniversary.

> Eesti koorilaul on ühendanud eestlased üheks rahvaks, kel üks süda ja üks meel, ja on saatnud eesti rahvuslikku ärkamist; ta ühendab meid ka paguluses, ta ei lase meid unustada me kodumaad, ta täidab me südamed võimsate kodumaa tunnetega ja süvendab meis usku Eesti vabaduse taasärkamisse.

> (The Estonian choral song has united Estonians into one nation with one heart and one mind, and has accompanied the Estonian national awakening; it also unites us in exile, it does not let us forget our homeland, it fills our hearts with powerful feelings of our homeland and deepens our faith in the hope of Estonia's freedom.)
>
> ("Eesti Segakoor", 1948)

Remembering the song festivals of the past and feeling enough hope to continue with choirs, was important to the DPs' resilience.

Was hope being lost amid the negative memories? There were certainly songs that focused on the sadness of exile. One song at the Geislingen 1946 concert was "Ei Mul Ole Isamaja" (I have no father's house). Hope was not such an easy commodity to find. One Estonian woman noted, "[M]y mouth is singing but the heart worries, and I am never entirely free from that" (Turno, 2004:86). Yet music has been shown to be an effective way of keeping hope alive and preserving memories. It has been found that "music helps people remember and/or learn about their heritage by functioning as a vehicle of memory" (Olson, 2004:3). Some immigrants may choose to use music to maintain their memories and hope, or they can choose to leave their memories behind. This is how choir director Aino Mägi explained the use of choirs to keep up hope and memories:

> [M]aybe the artistic merit of our singing was not very high, but we did our best considering the circumstances. My personal opinion is that we kept up our people's singing tradition and kept up the morale of Estonian refugees who had left behind all their worldly possessions.
>
> (Mägi, 1995)

At the 1947 Augsburg Song Festival, the tone was entirely hopeful, ending with "Laul Rõõmule" (Song of Rejoicing). At the end of the festival, the audience begged for the effervescent song about young love and marriage, "Tuljak," which the choir enthusiastically sang. The crowd left with a song full of uplifting hope ringing in their minds. L. Enari, the Geislingen Estonian Culture Committee Chair, wrote to the Geislingen choir, "Runo," on their third anniversary and expressed how much they represented hope for Estonians. "Väljendagu Teie laulud meie rahva muresid ja kannatusi aga ka tema rõõmusid, lootusi ja igatsusi. Kandku nad usku meie iseseisvuse ja vabaduse taassünnisse laiade hulkade südametesse" (may your songs express not just the sorrows and sufferings of our people, but also their joys, hopes, and longings. May they carry faith in the rebirth of our independence and freedom into the hearts of a large number) ("Eesti Segakoor," 1948)

Current Estonian President Kersti Kaljulaid knows that the hint of hope is important in song festivals even in times of freedom. At the 2019 Song Festival in Tallinn, she called for all to "sing with us with courage." She said the songs are "a glimmer of hope in every moment of sadness and a note of caution on even the happiest days" (July 4, 2019).

Identity and self-esteem

Singing in the choirs cemented memories and painted hope, which improved mood, increased confidence, and built a sense of identity and self-esteem. The impacts on self-esteem that singing brings about are recognizable. Researchers have found that for participants in choirs "singing improved their spirits and increased their levels of confidence and self-esteem. This may be related to the sense of achievement and fulfillment gained through practicing and making an improvement in performance" (Sanal, 2013:6). It appears that being in a choir could indeed be what helped the Estonians thrive, as research has shown that "singing in a choir had a significant impact on decreasing the negative affect and stated anxiety levels of singers." (Sanal, 2013:9).

The Estonians in the DP camp were still looking for family members that had been conscripted into service, been sent to Siberia, or been killed. They had left friends and family behind in Estonia and were not sure who survived the war. Knowing that they could not directly communicate with these loved ones, the use of music to communicate across boundaries was a powerful tool for identity. Loersch found that

> [m]usic is unique in its ability to transmit social information across distance to a number of people at once. Because of this, it allows a group to communicate without speech or direct interaction and, with the proper tools, enables this to happen across a much greater space than these other routes would allow. When participants' sense of belonging was threatened and they became motivated to reestablish social ties, they became more affected by the music they heard.
>
> (Loersch, 2013:15)

This communication without direct interaction was a powerful link to identity for the DPs as they sang their traditional songs. One of the most important song festival works is "Koit" by Lüdig, sung in 1969 at the 100th anniversary of first song festival (1869) and since then at every festival as the light is lit. In "Koit" (Dawn), the final two lines of lyrics by Estonian poet Friedrich Kuhlbars speak of the dawn of hope coming across the mountains:

> Mägede harjadel kumamas koit.
> Dawn breaks on the tops of the mountains.
> Taevasse tõusku me lootuse loit!
> May the flame of our hope soar to the heavens!

What was the Estonian identity? Not just a personal identity as one particular Estonian, but that identity as part of the larger Estonian community; as a member of the choir. It was the identity as a member of a singing nation. This way of "being an Estonian" is mentioned by many Estonian immigrants. When asked why she sings at song festivals, choir director Aino Mägi said,

> Estonians love music, already. You had to do something. Have to show something that you think is worth. You burst, you cannot hold it inside. You are like a kettle with too much steam. It piles up too much in you. I can't go just to work. It is in Estonian history when we had slavery they didn't kill our will to get better.
> (Mägi, 1991)

That is a powerful identity that provides vast, positive self-esteem.

Song festivals were an even more potent path to emotional and cultural resilience, as they required a high level of cooperation to organize. Choir singing in general already has been shown to promote trust (Anshel, 1988:152). The music of the song festival was not just a matter of singing together. It was singing very beautiful music, carefully prepared and with great skill *together*. This music is socially meaningful in part because it is so complex, involves so many people, and requires intense attention to be paid to detail to perform. This is where we can see how the song festivals in the DP camps, far from the Estonian homeland, did indeed become an important identifier for the Estonians in that "[m]usic styles can be made emblematic of national identities in complex and often contradictory ways" (Stokes, 1994:13).

While every culture has music, the identity formed in each culture is unique. While the population of Estonia was (and still is) small, the refugees had a large repertoire of their own music, and many Estonian composers and conductors had a heightened sense of what makes a song an Estonian song. Indeed, this is one of the things music can do—define a culture. Ethnomusicologist, Thomas Turino expertly explains this phenomenon:

> Musical sound comprises a large number of parameters occurring simultaneously – rhythm, meter, pitch series, key, mode instrumentation, quality of timbres, tempo, harmony texture, relative density, melodic shape, dynamics, musical quotes, and icons of 'extra-musical' sounds. The sonic events in each of these parameters may function independently as signs that parallel and support each other, conflict and thus create tension, or simply point to different things in new creative juxtapositions that function in ways similar to metaphor. In songs, texts using iconic, indexical, and symbolic language, as well as text-tune relationships, contribute additional resources for semiotic play and complex affects. In live performance a whole other realm of signs – facial expression, body motion, posture, physical articulation of the music an inner feeling – also become evident. Taken together, these elements make musical performance a particularly rich semiotic field that has the capability of producing particularly complex effects. As in all art, because of the nature of the artistic frame and because of the absence of strict grammars determining iconic and indexical semiotic combinations, music contains tremendous room for the creation of new coherent forms from pre-existing icons and indices. This is key for representing and articulating diasporic identities that are composites of elements from disparate social groups, locations, and types of experience.
>
> (Turino, 2004:17)

The repertoire of the song festivals in the DP camps included this complex composite of elements. The intricate choral compositions included old national songs, such as "Koit" by Lüdig, along with freshly minted compositions by those in the refugee camps. This intertwining of the repertoire helped build a new diasporic Estonian identity.

The song festivals were more complex than just being a concert of Estonian music. They were well-rehearsed and carefully planned public presentations of Estonia's musical culture. This is important in that "artistic practices have a special place in the realization and presentation of identity because they are usually framed as heightened forms of public presentation, practice and effects" (Turino, 2004:10). This importance of public impression is described in the Augsburg newspaper article, "Eesti laulupidu – suure moraalse jõu allikas" (The Estonian Song Celebration is the source of great moral power) (Eesti Rada, August 9, 1947). The writer explains,

> Laulupeod on Eesti areguloos olnud rahvusliku ühistunde kasvatajaks ja rahvusliku iseteadvuse õhutajaks. Laulupeod olid meie rahvale suureks moraalse jõu allikaks, mis õilsaid elamusi andes tiivustasid rahva hinge parematele püüdlustele, patriootilste ja esteetilis-eestiliste ideaalide suunas. Peame silmas pidama, et laulupidu peale sisemise tarviduse omab ka kaaluva välise tähenduse.
>
> (Song festivals have long been the breeding ground for national conscience and awakening of national identity in Estonia. Song festivals were a great source of moral power for our people, which, by giving proud experiences, drew the soul of the people to better aspirations, to the ideals of patriotic and artistic Estonians. We have to bear in mind that the song festival has not only an important inner, but also an important external meaning.)

Estonians in the DP camps had an effective vehicle to share their culture with others through the song festivals. This provided a communal sense of pride, identity, and self-esteem.

Preparing for the song festival and talking endlessly about it afterward were also important components of Estonian resilience. Each member of the audience, the choirs, and the organizing committee was proud to be part of something so beautiful. Estonian DP newspapers carried extensive stories outlining the events and discussing the most important features. Estonians treasured mementos from the song festivals and brought copies of the programs to their new homes in the United States, Canada, and Australia. They remembered each element of the Augsburg Song Festival as a key part of their story. Wong notes that music discourse is an elemental part of culture in that

> a nation can also be defined as a collection of people united (or fragmented) by the music they jointly listen to or debate about. These discourses create a frame of reference upon which people of different social and ethnic backgrounds position themselves within a national unit.
>
> (Wong, 2012:21)

Yes, even writing about and discussing the choirs and the song festivals gave the Estonian DPs a sense of identity and self-esteem in a time of great cultural upheaval.

Estonians in the DP camps had made an extraordinary transition. They had gone from being a newly independent culture to one spread from Soviet-controlled Estonia across a diaspora that included refugee camps. Upon realizing that returning to Estonia was not a viable option, DPs had to imagine how they could go on as immigrants. The choirs helped them imagine how such a change in identity could happen. Their process of change would have continuity because of their choirs.

> Music, then, functions as a lens—a lens through which snapshots of a people's "process of becoming" are seen in all their complexity. When the past and present are in question, the need to control the lens through which they are seen (and see themselves) becomes urgent and palpable. Music's flexibilities—its negotiable and permeable boundaries—allow it to traverse and prioritize the many layers that threaten and complicate a people's semblance of meaning.
> (Alajaji, 2013:256)

The song festivals were a way to meet the challenges of the transition and help in the process of becoming "Estonian American," "Estonian Canadian," and "Estonian Australian." There was no need to give up their hope, memories, and identities as Estonians. Estonians could sing their way into a new life while maintaining their resilient identity.

Refugees in every place, and in in every time, have suffered horrifically. International aid organizations provide for physical needs that are indeed desperate. Just as desperate as physical need, however, is the essential emotional need for resilience—that ability to thrive amid chaos and hardship. Estonian refugees spoke about this as a need for breathing, openness, flying, and/or freedom. Resilience is aided by a sense of hope, memories, identity, and self-esteem. Singing together in choirs does appear to facilitate this resilience. The Estonian choirs and song festivals after WWII gave Estonian refugees an opportunity to sing their way into a brighter future.

The Estonian diaspora: singing and preserving an identity in a new land

Some Estonian immigrants left Estonia before WWII and came to America to find adventure or claim land. Sometimes Estonians (such as this author's grandparents) already had children and felt they needed to escape conscription into the Russian army, which frequently crept across the border into Estonia. Unlike the Estonians who went to DP camps after WWII, these early Estonian Americans had no plans to return to Estonia. They had their children learn English, not Estonian, and changed names like Helmut Kolm to Harry Holmes. These early Estonian immigrants were not refugees and were in a very different psychological situation. The earlier Estonian immigrants were able to sponsor many of the Estonian DPs who later immigrated to the US after WWII. Estonians were also in Canada before WWII. Those communities sponsored many Estonian immigrants to Canada after the war and joined with the new arrivals to build choirs to celebrate in song festivals (Aun, 1985). Many of the early immigrants became more involved in the Estonian American and Estonian Canadian communities after the post WWII Estonians refugees came to the United States and Canada.

Post-WWII Estonians, on the other hand, left Estonia with the idea that they would remain Estonians and with the hopes of an eventual return to their homeland. Composer Juhan Aavik noted that "Estonian music lives on in exile, although a normal development and progress is impossible under the conditions of exile. It can exist thanks to the dedication and idealism of the musicians." (1961:12) Aavik, and many other Estonian immigrants (for example Roman Toi and Udo Kasemets), did keep Estonian music alive in exile through choirs and song festivals.

Choirs and song festivals in Estonia continued under Soviet control after WWII as well. Olt explains,

> [W]hat singing as a way of self-expression means to Estonians may be taken from the time immediately after the end of the Second World War, in 1945. In October, applications from prospective participants in the coming Song Festival of 1947 were invited, and in three months, despite the war devastation, some 20,000 singers announced their intention to come.
>
> (1980:29)

The Estonian Singers' Union song book described the sense of hope through song heritage even under Soviet control saying,

> Võitluses meie omakultuuri, iseteadvuse ning ühistunde vastu on kommunistlikud vallutajad juba aastaid püüdnud hävitada eesti rahvuslikku laulupärandit. Hoolimata rõhumisest ja tagakiusamisest elab aga eesti laul kodumaal edasi.
>
> (In the struggle for our own culture, self-consciousness and a sense of togetherness, communist conquerors have for years been trying to destroy the Estonian national song heritage. Despite the oppression and persecution, however, the Estonian song lives on in its homeland.) (Eesti Lauljate Liidu, 1948) However, "musical life, like everything else, was strictly and rigidly regimented, in a Communist spirit. True, great attention was paid to music,

> but all compositions had to conform to Communist ideology and methods and serve the goals of the Soviet regime and Communist propaganda.
>
> (Aavik, 1961:12)

For this reason, many more musicians continued to escape to the West. There are places where music has endured after great hardship under surprisingly difficult conditions. In Lebanon, for instance, it was found that

> after the genocide and the arrival of Armenians in Lebanon in the early 1920s, singing in choirs became the first art that flourished in the Armenian society. This is due to the fact that music, being a social art, adapts itself to all conditions of society, and through music individual and collective ideals can be expressed.
>
> (Artinian, 2009:133)

In the case of Native Americans who were forced into a distant boarding school (Chemawa, near Salem, Oregon), ethnomusicologist Parkhurst found that "Chemawa's musicians have gone on to demonstrate that particular quality of character that can often predict psychological wellness and social success later in life: resiliency" (2014:185). This capacity for resilience is "dynamic in nature, is not an either-or status, and is influenced by one's context and culture" (Goodman et al, 2018, 310). Certainly, choirs and song festivals can adapt to many different situations. In Estonia, under the Soviet rule, the effect of resilience through singing was also powerful (see the movie "Singing Revolution" for an overview of this). Choral music and song festivals provided resilience to Estonians under Soviet control as well as in the diaspora.

Estonian choirs formed not just in the German DP camps but everywhere that Estonians DPs resettled. In Sweden, Hans Lebert told of how

> [c]hoir-singing has always been an activity characteristic of Estonians. So it was in Sweden as well. Already in 1948 an Estonian song festival was organized in Stockholm's nature park in Skansen. After the Skansen song festival I joined the Youth Choir. I was 24 years old. The choir director was Olav Roots, the legendary conductor of the Estonian Radio Symphony orchestra.
>
> (Hinrikus, 2009:275)

Meta Noorkukk, Augsburg DP camp choir director, emigrated to New York and started the NY Estonian women's choir. Many Estonian choirs formed in Canada, such as those directed by Roman Toi. Estonian choirs were founded in Australia, such as the men's choir in Sydney, directed by Edgar Siimpoeg. Madisson reminds us that "once landed in our adoptive countries choirs again sprang up. The voice box needed no space in the baggage" (2015:42). The first edition of "Various Songs" (1940) was published in Estonia just before the Soviet takeover. When it was republished in New York in 1948, the Estonian Aid society noted how important the small book was for promoting Estonian singing, social gatherings, and introducing Estonians as a singing culture in their new country (1948).

As Estonians emigrated around the world, with many going to the United States, Canada, Sweden, and Australia, the diaspora was growing with choirs everywhere. Music allows "permeable boundaries so that a group can re-consider their place in the world" (Stokes, 2003:213), so a diasporic people, such as this global Estonian community, can let the music translate their multiple worlds. The new music of a diaspora (Estonian as well as others) has many issues to consider:

> [I]dentity in music becomes a matter of boundaries. Issues dealt with, consciously or not, in the music of diasporas, include 'what is ours?'; 'what is not?'; 'what of theirs will we allow'; and 'what will we not?' The shift from boundary construction to boundary maintenance and boundary erosion speak not only to the processual nature of diaspora but also, as traced here, to the ways in which music contributes to this process.
>
> (Alajaji, 2013:240)

The Estonians asked these questions and the answers included: "Choirs are Estonian" and "Song festivals are Estonian."

On the West Coast of North America, Estonian choirs formed in Los Angeles, San Francisco, Portland, Seattle, and Vancouver, BC. The Eesti Insenerkompanii Meeskoor (Estonian Engineering Company men's choir from Geislingen) conductor Rein Neggo started a mixed choir in Los Angeles (which was later led by Jaak Kukk). In Seattle, Aino Mägi, choir director and singer in the DP camps, started a mixed choir and women's choir. Zoja Vaga started a choir in Portland in 1951, which she directed for 40 years before turning the baton over to Kati Tamm.

These choirs included many of the singers who had performed in the song festivals in WWII DP camps. Many of the Estonians who had moved to the West Coast of America had been friends in Estonia and had lived together in the DP camps. They began to look for ways to keep in touch and to visit with these friends. Even more important, they were looking for ways to preserve their cultural memories in the hopes of a return to Estonia.

Song festivals logically held importance to the Estonians in the diaspora, with both pre- and post-WWII emigres, as a way to preserve their memories and to celebrate their hopes of returning to Estonia. On the West Coast of the Americas, several Estonian communities decided that a combined West Coast Estonian League could provide a stronger ethnic identity and, of course, would include song festivals. The first Lääneranniku Eesti Päevad (LEP: West Coast Estonian Days) was held in San Francisco during Labor Day weekend 1953. The first West Coast Estonian Days included groups from California and Oregon. The first meeting, and all those that have followed, include a song festival as a key event along with dance, sports, and theatre. The LEP events soon added groups from Seattle, Washington, and Vancouver, British Columbia. The West Coast Estonian Days, which are held approximately every other summer, have been located in San Francisco: 1953, 1959, 1967, 1975, 1983, 1993, 2001, 2013; Los Angeles: 1955, 1963, 1971, 1979, 1989, 1999, 2007, 2017; Portland: 1957, 1965, 1973, 1985, 1995, 2003, 2011, 2019; Vancouver: 1961, 1969, 1977, 1987, 1997, 2005, 2015 (at Whistler), and Seattle 1981, 1991, 2009, 2022.

The first West Coast Estonian Days were initially intended to preserve Estonian culture and to prepare refugees to be ready to return home. The event has also helped the community remain resilient when the return home to Estonia appeared to be a less-than-plausible goal. Estonians who came from the DP camps talked about the importance of the song festivals in camps and in later festivals as "a way to remind [us] we are still something" and "to show that we are still here" (Mägi, 1991) and "we existed and that we still exist" (Shuey, 1991). The Seattle Post Intelligencer quoted Seattle Estonian August Raja in explaining why the event is so important: "We've always been a battleground for the major European powers. And the song festivals, or 'Laulupidu', which began in 1869, have continued to be the historic tradition embodying the Estonian national identity" (July 27, 1981:A3). After Estonia regained freedom with the collapse of the Soviet Union in 1991, there was considerable attention within the Estonian diaspora as to the changing role of the West Coast Estonian

Days. Kaskla noted the change as "the entire raison d'etre had been to draw attention to the plight of an occupied country so small that it was mostly ignored, now it was about how to support Estonia and what it meant culturally to be Estonian" (Kaskla, 2020:21). The song festivals do still bring together the Estonian community as before. Amid the 2020 COVID pandemic, Seattle Estonians continue to prepare for the 2022 LEP festival, which remains on hold until the group can meet together safely.

Preparing the 2011 Laulupidu (song festival) in free Estonia, the organizers wrote,

> To quote Gustav Ernesaks: 'The Estonian people have never known how to live without singing.' Each choir member contributes his talents to support the tradition of Estonian choral music and, undoubtedly, cannot conceive of a day without song. However one defines the spirit, it is present in our voices.
>
> (Eesti Organisatsioonide Liit Läänarannikul)

That same spirit and resilience was present in each of the West Coast Estonian Days. Even though there are now song festivals in free Estonia, the tradition lives on in the United States and Canada as a cultural icon of Estonians in the diaspora.

The international Estonian diaspora organized "ESTO" in 1972, beginning with the Toronto, Canada ESTO celebration. This event was originally designed to maintain Estonian culture and language during the Soviet occupation of Estonia. The festivals have been held every four years, even after Estonian independence, as an opportunity to celebrate the culture and heritage of Estonia. These ESTO festivals have been hosted by Toronto: 1972, 1984, 2000; Baltimore: 1976; Stockholm: 1980; Melbourne: 1988; New York: 1992; Stockholm-Tallinn: 1996; Riga: 2004; Münster: 2009; San Francisco: 2013; and Helsinki-Tartu: 2019. A key element of each ESTO is the song festival. Instead of having a festival in 2017, that date was moved to 2019 to coincide with the 150-year celebration of the very first song festival and to coincide with the song festival in Tallinn.

The festivals in free Estonia and around the Estonian diaspora continue to emphasize the absolute core necessity for Estonians to sing in choirs and song festivals. The Estonian Song Festivals (as well as those in Latvia and Lithuania) are on the UNESCO list of "Oral and Intangible Cultural Heritage of Humanity" (November 2013 designation). All Baltic communities (Estonian, Latvian, and Lithuanian) use choral music as a self-identifier and way to promote their cultures.

Baltic scholar Rimvydas Šilbajoris wrote of this Baltic identity linked to song festivals, saying,

> [A] meadowlark by the sea, making all the heavens sing in Estonian, Latvian and Lithuania, has not heard from his Maker that at the beginning was the word, but his song is true to itself and therefore does speak clearly to the soul. As scholars, we do not much resemble a meadowlark; yet, we also yearn for something that is free and true, and so, our need is essentially the same- to sustain our identity and integrity by our very being, thus acquiring the power to serve truth as fact and also as vision.
>
> (Šilbajoris (1995, 1)

The use of the song festival to aid identity formation is central to the culture in all three Baltic countries.

Song festivals continue to be a source of resilience for Estonians in Estonia and abroad. President Kersti Kaljulaid spoke to the song festival audience July 4, 2019 about the importance of song, saying, "Song brings Estonians joy. Song gives Estonians courage. Song makes Estonians free." The organizers of the ongoing song festivals in Estonia are aware of the importance of these festivals as deeply rooted emblems of Estonian identity. In the program from the 2009 song festival, *To Breathe as One*, the organizers wrote:

> It is not a coincidence that in the Estonian language the words "soul" and "breathing" come from the same stem. One word developed from the other, because breathing and soul are connected. Even so closely connected that if you breathe in the same rhythm with someone, with a little luck it is possible to see his soul. The same magic works when tens and thousands breathe as one. They look for the right place in a hurry, gasping for breath. They hold their breath in anticipation. They rejoice from their heart and soul. This is when the soul of one nation meets. It is breathtakingly beautiful. By breathing as one, history can be changed. The vibrations of the soul create a resonance that has broken iron and brought down political regimes. But it is not the only aim of breathing as one. This celebration unites us with those who sang and danced before us, as well as with our contemporaries whose soul may go unnoticed in the everyday rat race. When people breathe as one, it does not matter whether you face the audience of the performers or whether you are somewhere else instead. When you breathe with others as one, your soul is there.

Breathing as one—this level of choral participation is indeed central to Estonian spirit and has provided hope, memories, and identity that provide the resilience needed to survive against all odds. When the COVID-19 pandemic hit Estonians, along with the rest of the world, the Estonian response was again to sing. The Eesti Kooriühing (Estonian Choir Association) stated, "Until today, we cannot meet. But this common feeling is needed by the people and must be amplified. It gives strength" (https://kooriyhin.ee/tule-laulma-eriolukorra-lopulaulu/). The choirs of Estonia called Estonians everywhere to join in song. As the state of emergency was finally lifted in Estonia, the country celebrated with a virtual song festival. A virtual choir of 2,500 singers sang *Isamaa ilu hoieldes* (Preserving the Beauty of the Homeland) by Alo Matiisen. The virtual choir was live streamed in the Tallinn Song Festival grounds, with an enormous screen full of the combined virtual singers, a live band, a live conductor, and people in cars of no more than one household each. They sang together a song of hope and honked horns and cheered at the end (see https://estonianworld.com/culture/virtual-choir-to-celebrate-the-end-of-the-emergency-in-estonia/). The concert was live streamed on ERR, the Estonian public broadcaster.

Estonians have endured countless difficulties before and after World War II. The Estonian song festivals in the post WWII DP camps were critical in helping store memories, reinstate hope, and support a sense of Estonian identity. Music provided a unique way to focus on memories and hope through choirs and song festivals. These song festivals also promoted a sense of community and a common identity. This singing together in choirs and song festivals has indeed provided resilience for the Estonians in Estonia, as refugees, in foreign-controlled Estonia, in the diaspora, and in free Estonia.

‖: The song goes on:‖.

Appendix A
Estonian choral music timeline

1637	Estonian Lutheran hymnal published.
1778	Herder included Estonian song in *Volkslieder.*
1816	Serfdom abolished in Estonia.
1869	Carl Jakobsen published collection of Estonian folk song arrangements.
1869	Song Festival I held in Tartu as part of the national movement towards independence, the Time of Awakening.
1879	Song Festival II held in Tartu.
1880	Song Festival III held in Tallinn Kadriog Park.
1891	Song Festival IV held in Tartu.
1894	Song Festival V in Tartu.
1896	Song Festival VI held in Tallinn (as are all of the rest).
1905	Revolution in Russia.
1910	Song Festival VII.
1914–1918	World War I.
1918 Feb	German occupation of Estonia.
1918 Nov–1920 Jan	War of Independence. Estonians declare independence. Estonian forces beat back German and Soviet armies—aided at critical points by the British.
1920 Feb	The Treaty of Tartu. The treaty between Russian and Estonia recognized Estonian independence.
1923	Song Festival: The first festival in free Estonia with an all-Estonian repertoire.
1928	Song Festival IX in present-day Tallinn song festival grounds.
1933	Song Festival X.
1938	Song Festival XI.
1939–1945	World War II.

1939 Feb	Hitler and Stalin divided Europe into spheres of influence, with the Baltics left to the Soviets.
1939	Soviet Union forced Estonia to accept Soviet military bases.
1940 Jun	Soviet troops invaded Estonia.
1940 Aug	Estonia forcibly incorporated into Soviet Union.
1941 Jun 14	First mass deportations of Estonians by the NKVD (Soviet secret police).
1941–1944	Germany invaded Estonia followed by German occupation.
1944	Estonia invaded again by the Soviet Union. Tens of thousands of Estonians deported to Siberia and Central Asia. Soviet re-occupation of Estonia.
1946	Summer Days Estonian Displaced Person Concert in Geislingen, Germany.
1947	Song Festival XII in occupied Estonia. Unofficial anthem by Gustav Ernesaks emerged.
1947 Aug. 9/10	Augsburg Song Festival in Estonian DP camp in American Zone of Germany.
1948	Estonian DP camp song festival in Kempten.
1949	Second mass deportation of Estonians (by Soviets).
1950	Song Festival XIII in occupied Estonia.
1953	First West Coast Estonian Days (LEP) held in San Francisco.
1955	Song Festival XIV in occupied Estonia.
1960	Song Festival XV in occupied Estonia.
1965	Song Festival XVI in occupied Estonia.
1969	Song Festival XVII in occupied Estonia.
1972	ESTO international song festival for Estonian diaspora held in Toronto, Canada.
1975	Song Festival XVIII in occupied Estonia.
1980	Song Festival XIX in occupied Estonia.
1985	Song Festival XX in occupied Estonia. Perestroika announced by Soviet government.
1987	First open anti-Soviet protest in Estonia, with popular protests held against Soviet plans for open-cast mining of phosphorus in Estonia.
1988	Estonian-Soviet legislature declared sovereignty. Popular front for independence dubbed the "Singing Revolution" because peaceful rallies usually included singing.

1989 Aug	Baltic Way (also known as Baltic Chain), where over 2 million people formed a human chain connecting each Baltic capital in Estonia, Latvia, and Lithuania.
1990	Transition to independence declared by Soviet-Estonian legislature.
1990	Song Festival XXI as Singing Revolution begins to melt occupation. Soviet songs and propaganda replaced with Estonian repertoire and national symbols.
1991 Jan	Soviet crackdown on Baltic States.
1991 Aug	Coup in the Kremlin attempted but failed. Since Moscow's authority collapsed, the dream of restoring independence came true.
1991	Estonia joined United Nations and the KGB ended its operations in Estonia.
1992	Currency change—Estonia replaced the Russian Ruble with the Estonian Crown (Kroon).
1993	Estonia started to privatize state-owned businesses.
1994	Russian army left Estonia.
1994	Song Festival XXII celebrated 125 years since the first edition.
1998	Estonia started negotiations to join the European Union.
1999	Song Festival XXIII.
2003	SKYPE developed in Estonia.
2003	Estonian song and dance festivals included in the UNESCO's List of the Intangible Cultural Heritage of Humanity.
2004 Mar 29	Estonia accepted into NATO. It was the first time in its history that Estonia joined a military alliance voluntarily.
2004 May 1	Estonia joined the European Union.
2004	Song Festival XXIV, Theme: "Always on the Road" preceded by planting of communal forest.
2009	Song Festival XXV with joint choirs of more than 25,000 singers and 7,500 dancers participating, Theme: "To Breathe as One."
2014	Song Festival XXVI with over 42,000 singers, Theme: "Touched by Time. The Time to Touch."
2019	Song Festival XXVII, 150th anniversary of the first song festival and 85th anniversary of dance festival, Theme: "Minu Arm" (My Love).

2020	Estonian Choir Association virtual choir celebration of COVID state of emergency being lifted.
2024	Song Festival XXVIII will be held again in Tallinn.

Appendix B
Maps

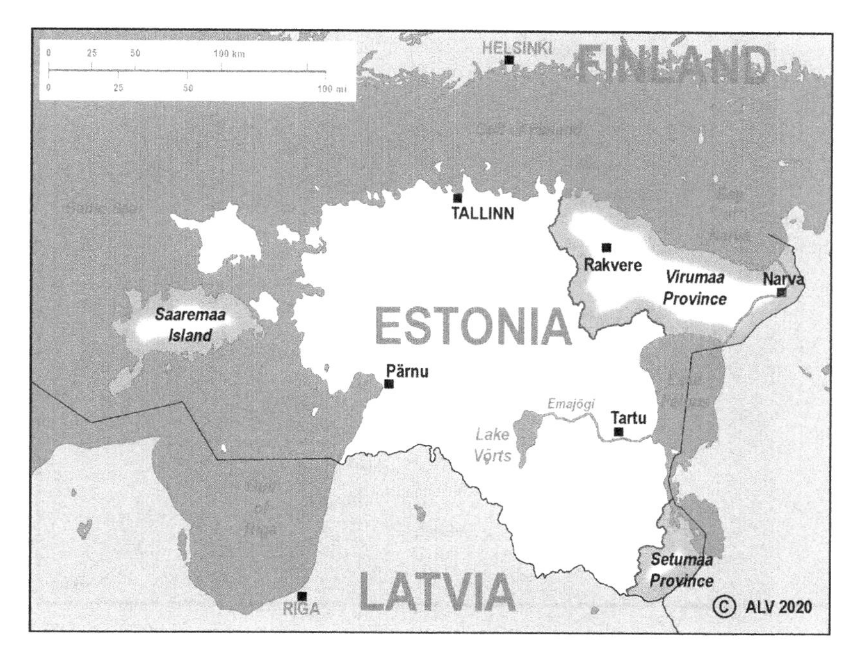

Figure B.1 Map of Estonia with locations mentioned in book. Map by Arvo Vercamer, 2020.

Figure B.2 Map of Estonian DP Camps in Germany, 1945–1952. Map by Arvo Vercamer, 2020.

Appendix C
List of repertoire from camps

List derived from DP concert programs from Estonian Archives in Australia and IHRCA

April 1 and 2, 1946 Geislingen mixed choir, Meeme Mälgi director

May 3, 1946, Geislingen, men's choir, Maniwald Loite director

August 2, 3, and 4, 1946 Geislingen, men's choirs and mixed choirs (directors Anton Kasemets, Adalbert. Virkhaus, Roman Toi, Meeme Mälgi, and E. Reebs)

November 30 and Dec. 3, 1946 Geislingen men's choir, Roman Toi director

February 24, 1947 Estonian independence concert, mixed choir and children's choir, Kempten, Albert Pruks directingFebruary 28, 1947 Estonian Mixed choir concert in Hanau with choirs from Augsburg, Kempten, and Hanau, directors Meta Tari-Noorkukk (Augsburg), Albert Pruks (Kempten), and August Pruul, (Hanau)

June 12, 1947 Kempten mixed choir, Albert Pruks director

** August 10, 1947 Augsburg Song Festival, head conductors, Anton Kasemets, Udo Kasemets, Roman Toi and August Pruul. Note: Compositions from this program are marked (A47) in the repertoire list below.

September 28, 1947 Mixed choirs from Augsburg, Kempten, Hanau (directors- Meta Tari-Noorkukk, Albert Pruks, August Pruul)

November 29 and 30, 1947 men's choir, Geislingen, Roman Toi director

February 24, 1948 Geislingen mixed choir (Udo Kasemets director) and men's choir (Roman Toi director)

February 24, 1948 Kempten mixed choir Albert Pruks director

March 26, 1948 Geislingen men's choir, Roman Toi director

July 3, 1948 Women's choir, Augsburg, Meta Noorkukk director
September 26, 1948, Kempten, song festival, men's choir, mixed choir
May 8, 1949 Choir and Orchestra Concert, Stuttgart Philharmonic (Dr. W. van Hoogstraten, director) and Estonian Men's choir of Geislingen (Roman Toi, director)
July 2, 1949 Lingen mixed choir, August Ruut director
September 18, 1949 Lingen mixed choir performing in Oldenburg
September 30, 1949 Lingen choir performing in Lingen gymnasium, August Ruut director
October 10, 1949 Lingen mixed choir performing in Greven, August Ruut director
(A47) denotes a composition that was performed at the 1947 Augsburg Song Festival

Mixed choir (Segakoor)

Aav, Evald	Murelaul
	Laulik (uses common regilaul text"kui mina hakkan laulemaie")
Aavik, Juhan	Meie laulame (A47)
	Kodutee
	Noorte laul
Ernesaks, Gustav	Hakkame, mehed minema
Hagfors, E.	Laul Imatrale (A47)
Hermann, K.A.	Troostilaul
Hoppe, R.	Laulab minu laululind
Horwath, A.	Sügisel
Härma, Miina	Enne ja nüüd
	Kojuigatsus
	Tuljak
	Tule koju
	Veel kaitse kange Kalev (A47)
Jürme, J.	Rukkiräk
Kalnins, A.	Hümn Latviale (A47)
Kapp, Artur	Mu süda (A47)
	Ei eksi
	Palumine
Kapp, Eugen	Mets
Kasemets, Udo	Oi sünnimaa (A47)
	Me Tuleme
Kuula, T.	Nuiameeste mars

Känd, Herman	Kaugel (A47)
Loigu, Valdeko	Möök varastatakse
	Jutegija
Läte, Aleksander.	Ärka üles, isamaa (A47)
	Kostke laulud Eesti keeles
	Kui on kadund
	Laul röömule (A47)
Lüdig, Mihkel.	Karjase laul
	Koit (Dawn).
	Laevnik (A47)
	Laulud nüüd lähevad
	Sääl kord kasvab
Mandre, Jüri	Ei kesta igavesti vägivald
	Vabadus vöidab
Merikanto-Vettik	Kui tuli tumeneb
Oja, Eduard	Kangakudumise laul
Melngailis, E.	Tutiline linnukene
	Kägu kukub
Päts, Riho	Lopna laul
	Sangarite laul
	Pulmalaul
Rootsi Viis	Rõõmsad muusikandid
Saar, Mart.	Ainult pale virju
	Põhjavaim (A47)
Simm, Juhan.	Oma saar
Säbelmann, F.	Palve
Strolia, J.	Leedu Laul (A47)
Tobias, R.	Varas
Türnpuu, Konstantin	Kevade tunne
	Ei mul ole isamaja
	Lahkumise laul
	Mul lapsepölves rääkis
	Mu armas isamaa
	Priiuse hommikul
Vedro, Adolf	Midrilinnu mäng
Vettik, Tuudur	Kas tunned maad (A47)
	Mu Sünnimaa
	Su põhjamaa päikese kullast (A47)
	Teid ma tervitan
Virkhaus, Adelbert	Tuisk
Vörk, Enn	Eesti Lipp

	Helise ilma (A47)
	Lauljate lipulaul
	Lilleside
	Looja vägevus

Women's choir (Naiskoor)

Aavik, Juhan	Kodu (A47)
	Mälestus
Ernesaks, Gustav	Noor kevede
	Hannikainen Suve õhtu
Härma, Miina	Küll oli ilus mu õieke
	Tuljak
Kunileid, Aleksander	Sind surmani
Läte, Aleksander	Kuld rannake
Saar, Mart	Tipa-tapa hällilaul
Türnpu, Konstantin	Tervitus (A47)
	Lauluke
Vedro, A.	Midrilinnu mäng (A47)
Vettik, Tuudur	Mu sünnimaa (A47)
	Kuu
Virkhaus, Adalbert	Laula, laula suuke
Võrk, Enn	Ärge unustage
	Naabri Mari

Men's Choir (Meeskoor)

Aav, Evald	Humal (A47)
Aavik, Juhan.	Kojuigatsus
Aave, E.	Nooruse aeg
Blieve, J.	Oode
Enno, Ernst	Igatsus
	Tipa-tapa hällilaul
Ernesaks, Gustav.	Hakkame mehed minema
Härma, Miina.	Meeste laul
	Tuljak
Karlson, Ferdinand	Ela Eesti!
Kasemets, Anton Ju	kumab koit (A47)
Kuhlbars, Friedrich	Kaugel
Kuula, T.	Nuiameeste mars
Känd, H.	Kaugel
Liiv, Juhan	Üle vee
Lilleleid Loigu, Valdeko	Löpp ja algus (A47)

Läte, Aleksander	Kuldrannake (A47)
Oja, Eduard	Me olime nagu lapsed
Palmgren, S.	Miilipöletaja
Päts, Riho	Jaan läeb jaanitulele
Rahvalaul	Leelo
Ridala, V.	Talvine õhtu Hall Laul
Setu viis	Lätsi küllä Simm, Juhan Mulgimaale
Sööt, Karl	Aimdus
Suits, G.	Mehed
	Nooruse aeg
	Oma saar
Talvik, Heiti	Lahingu ratsud
Toi, Roman	Ela Eesti
	Pea vastu (A47)
Torro, Karl	Karmis ajas
Türnpu, Konstantin	Helju, hella tuulekene
	Ei mul ole isamaja
	Meil aiaäärne tanaval
	Mu armas isamaa
	Mu Eestimaa
	Mul lapsepölves rääkis (A47)
	Tervitus
Vörk, Enn	Isamaale
	Ma lillesideme vötaks

Children's choir (Lastekoor)

Suits, G.	Kevade Laul

Appendix D

Handwritten scores used in camps

Scores from Aino Mägi

Figure D.1 Hermann, K.A. "Murnamäel," handwritten with blue ink on very thin orange paper with a second verse added in purple ink.

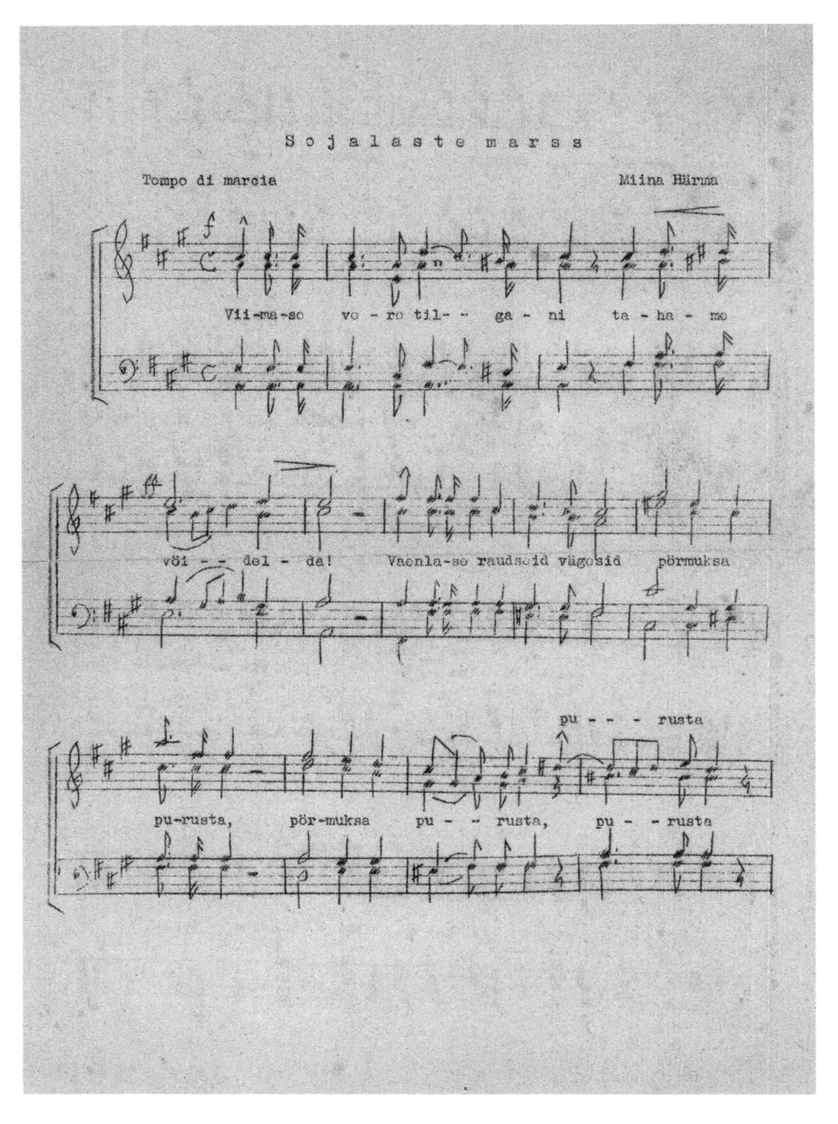

Figure D.2 Härma, Miina. "Söjalaste marss," hand-notated and typed lyrics. Black ink on two sides of tan paper. Front page only.

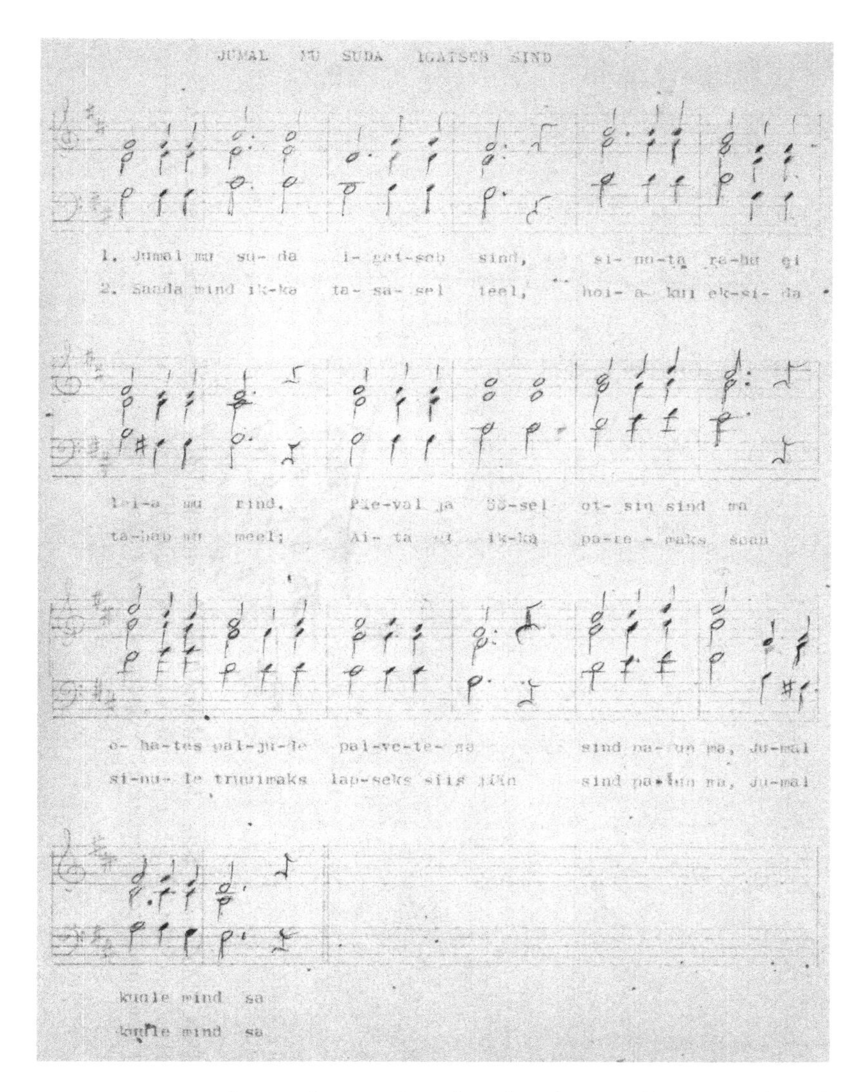

Figure D.3 "Jumal mu süda igatseb sind," a hand-notated hymn in blue ink on tan paper with lyrics typed below.

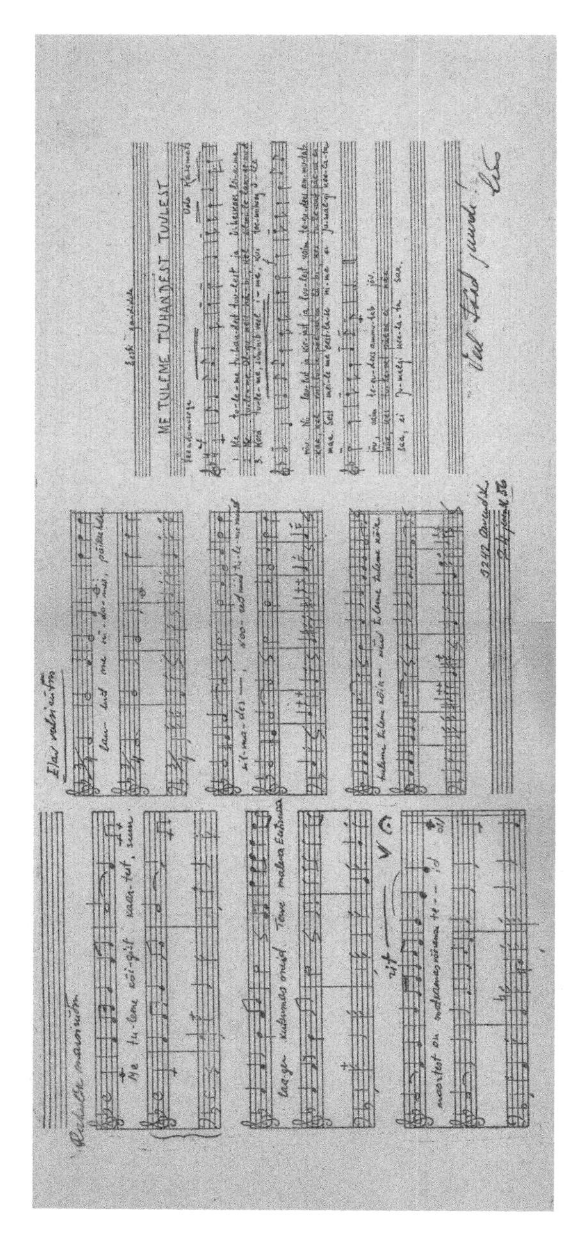

Figure D.4 Kasemets, Udo. “Me Tuleme Tuhandest Tuulest,” handwritten black ink on brown paper, long rectangle (5 by 11) signed “Veel tööd juurde! Udo” by composer and choir director Kasemets. On same sheet there are two excerpts of other pieces that appear to be variations, including a waltz version.

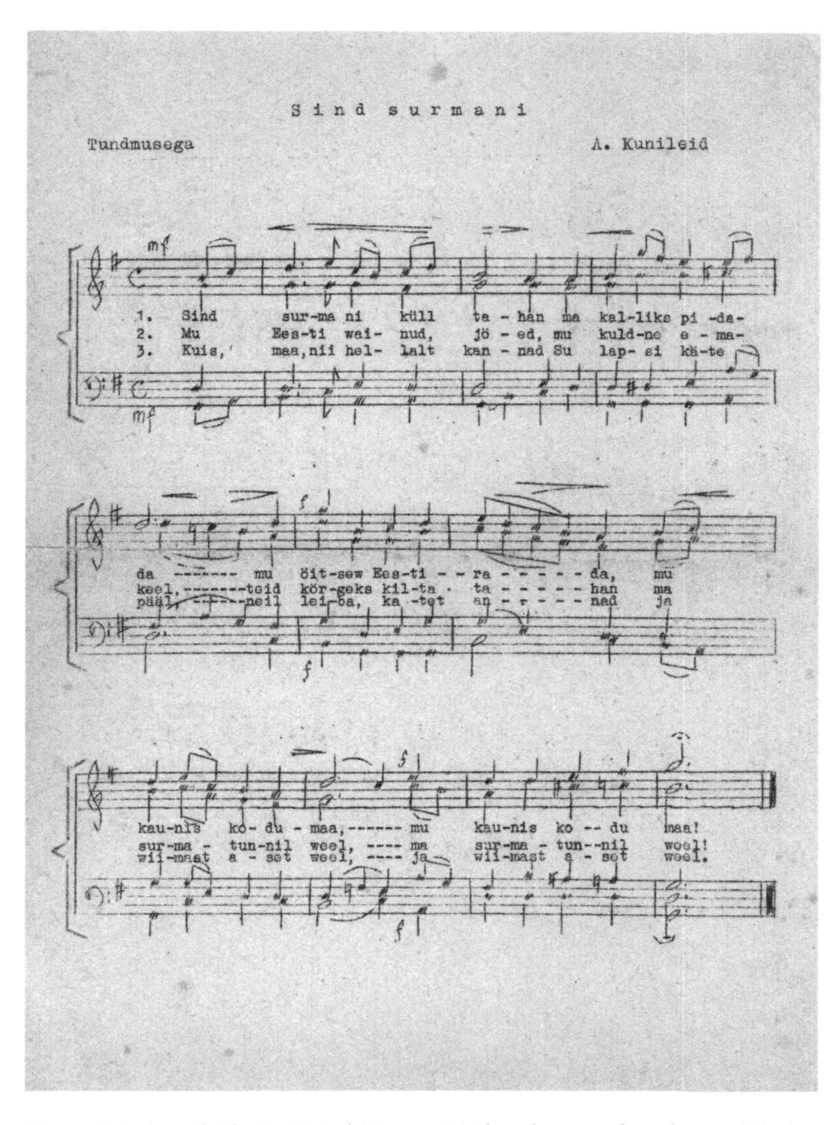

Figure D.5 Kunileid, A. "Sind Surmani," hand-notated and typed lyrics. Black ink on two sides of tan paper going on to third page that ends with the lyricist's name, Lydia Koidula. Front page only.

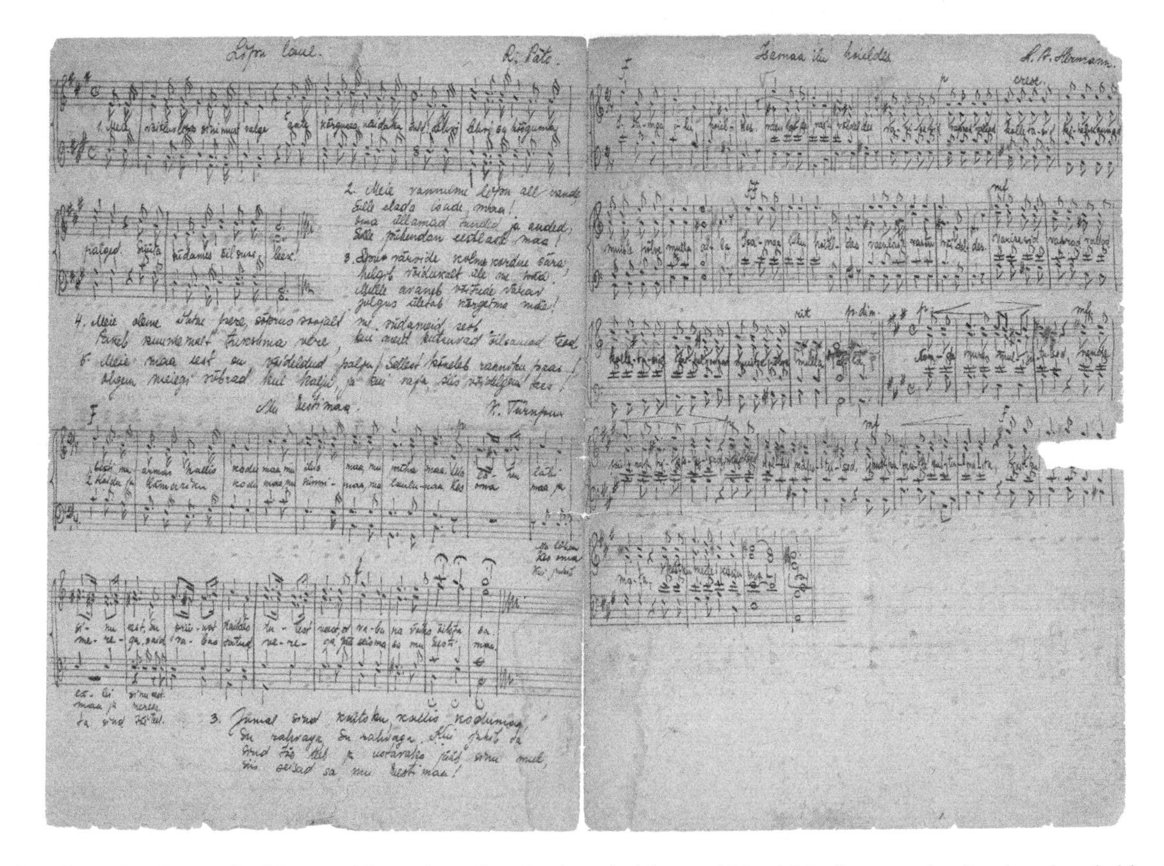

Figure D.6 Päts, R. "Lopna laul," one of four pieces handwritten in blue on 11 by 20 inch paper that has handmade blue/purple staves.

Figure D.7 "Pulmalaul" Eesti rahvaviis (Estonian folk song). Handwritten blue ink on orange/tan thin paper in Aino Mägi's handwriting.

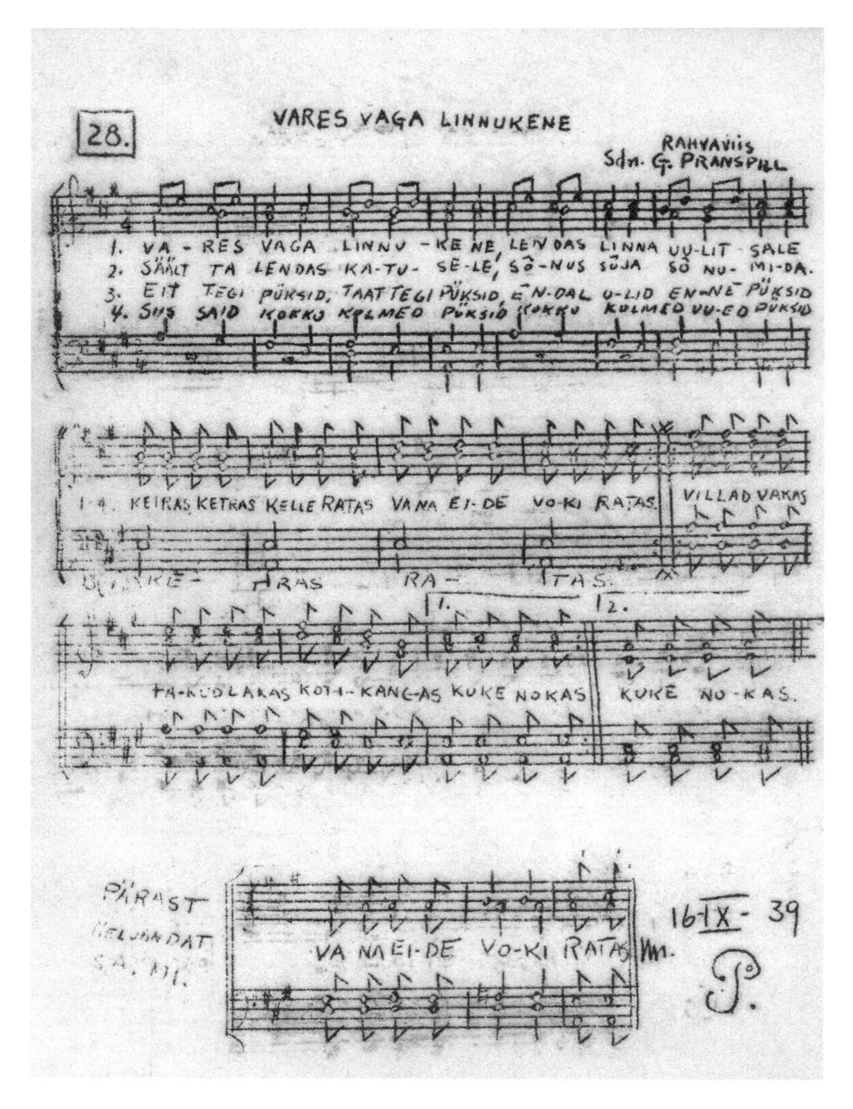

Figure D.8 Pransipal, G. (rahvaviis) "Vares Vaga Linnukene." Number 28 in box on upper left. Hand-printed and notated with black ink on tan paper. Signed P 16-IX-1939. Probably written in Estonia before Pransipal left the country. Aino Mägi would have had it with her in the Geislingen camp.

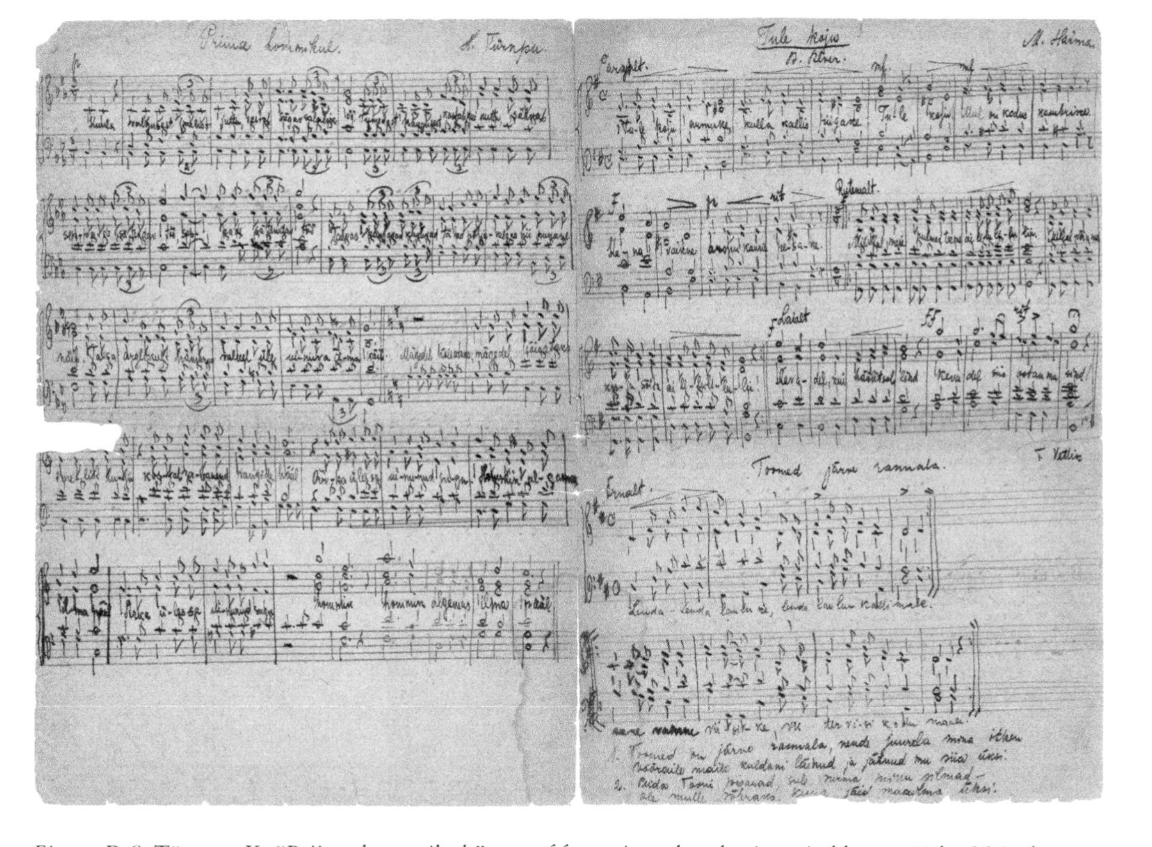

Figure D.9 Türnpu, K. "Priiuse hommikul," one of four pieces handwritten in blue on 11 by 20 inch paper that has handmade blue/purple staves.

Scores from Inno Salasoo

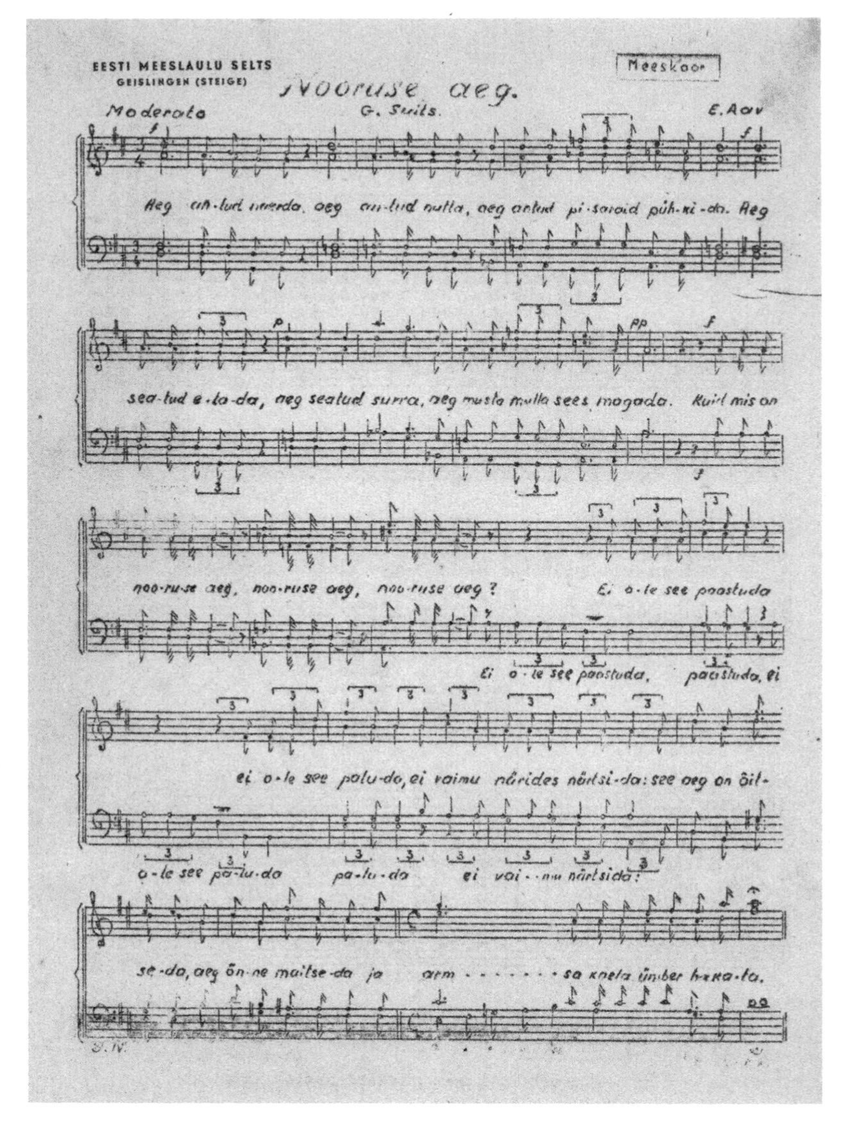

Figure D.10 Aav, E. “Nooruse aeg” (G. Suits), Eesti Meeslaulu Selts (Estonian Men’s Choir Organization) Geislingen (Steige), black mimeograph on tan paper on the back side of “Lauliku Kodu.”

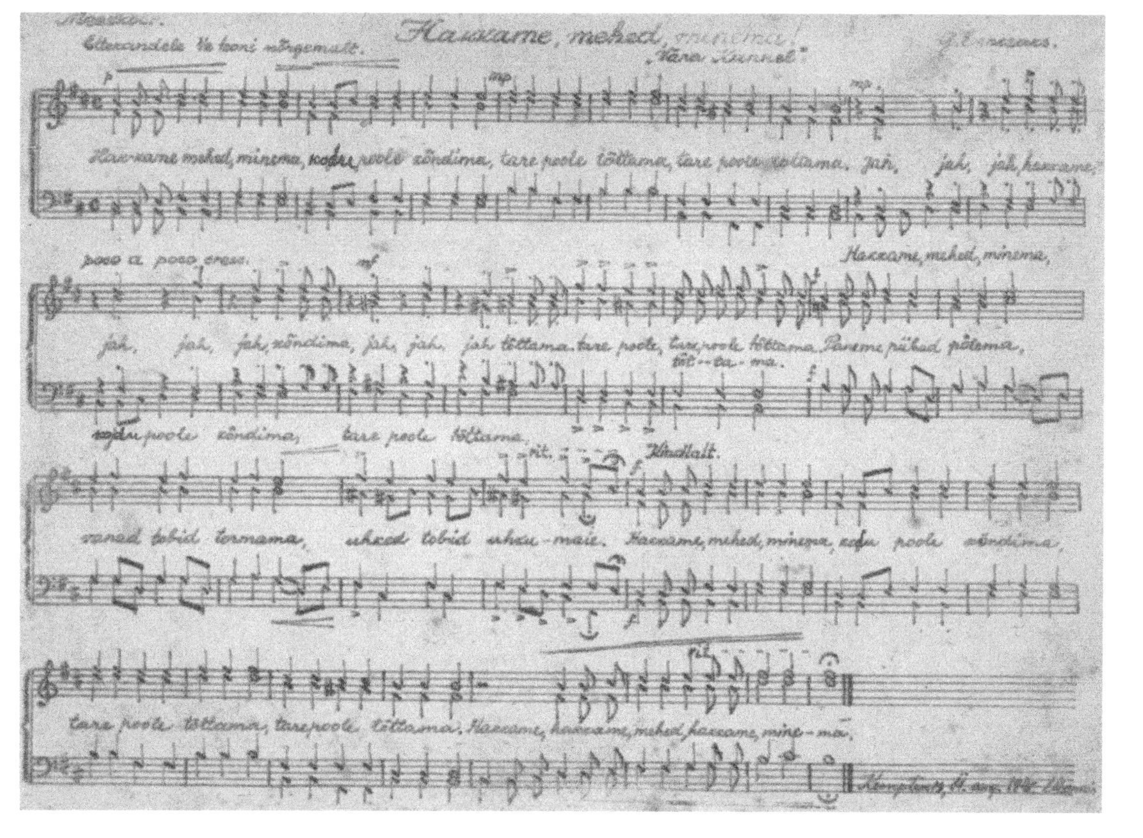

Figure D.11 Ernesaks, Gustav. “Hakkame, mehed minemal: Vana Kannel” for men’s choir. Handwritten in blue ink on tan paper in Kempten, August 11, 1947 by L. Mankin, on the back side of another handwritten “Laviumise laul.”

Figure D.12 Härma, M. "Veel kaitse, kange Kalev" Blue ink on tan paper, follow last three measures on the back side and then "Eesti Lipp." Kempten November 25, 1945, by Albert Pruks. Pruks died of cancer in Geislingen in 1948.

Figure D.13 Oja, Ed. “Kangakudumise laul,” handwritten mixed choir, brown ink on tan paper. Front page only.

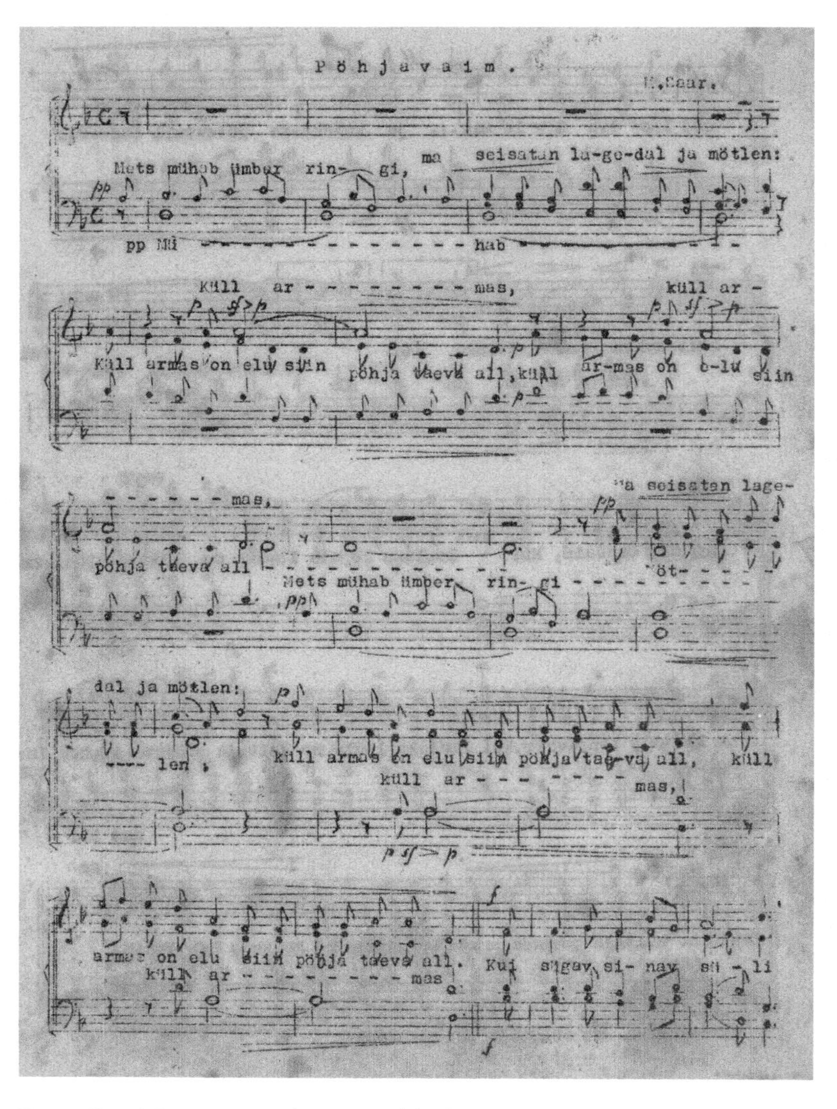

Figure D.14 Saar, M. "Pöhjavaim," black typing with hand notation on tan paper.

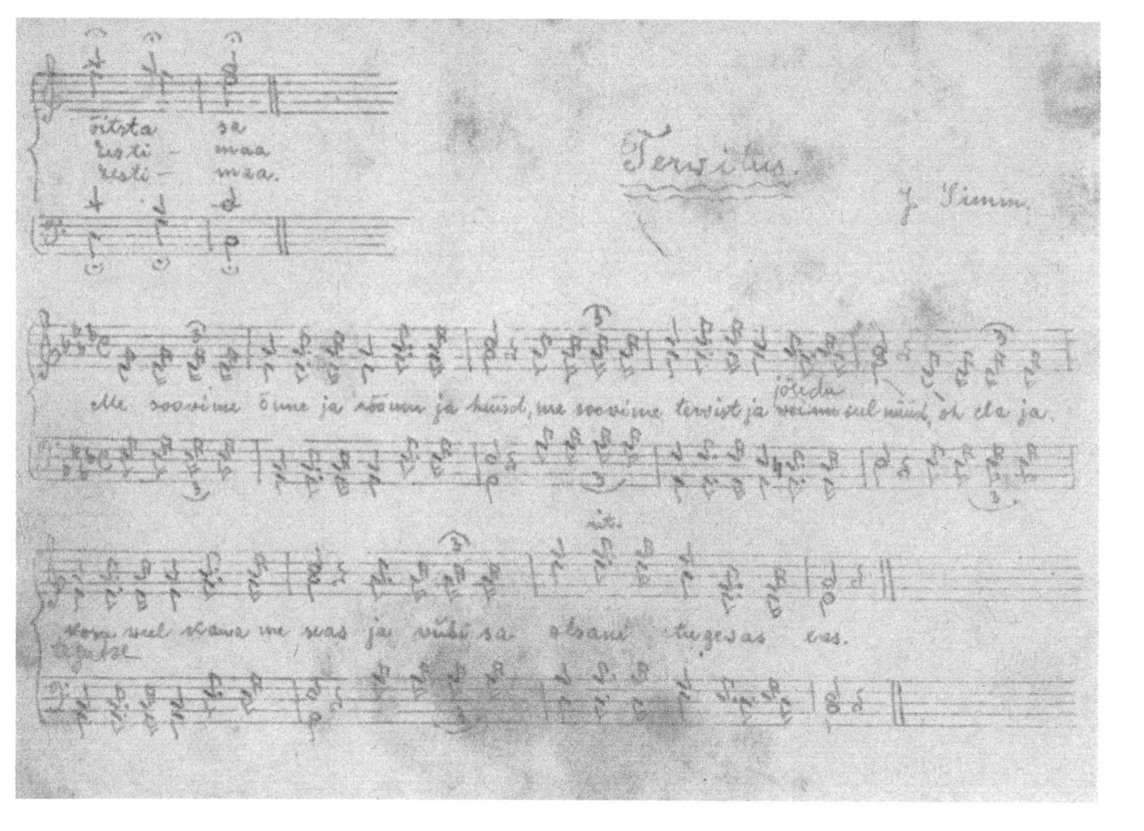

Figure D.15 Simm, J. "Tervitus," handwritten in blue ink on small (5 by 8½ inch) tan paper, the last two bars of "Mu Eestmaa" on top and then "Mu Eestimaa" on the back side.

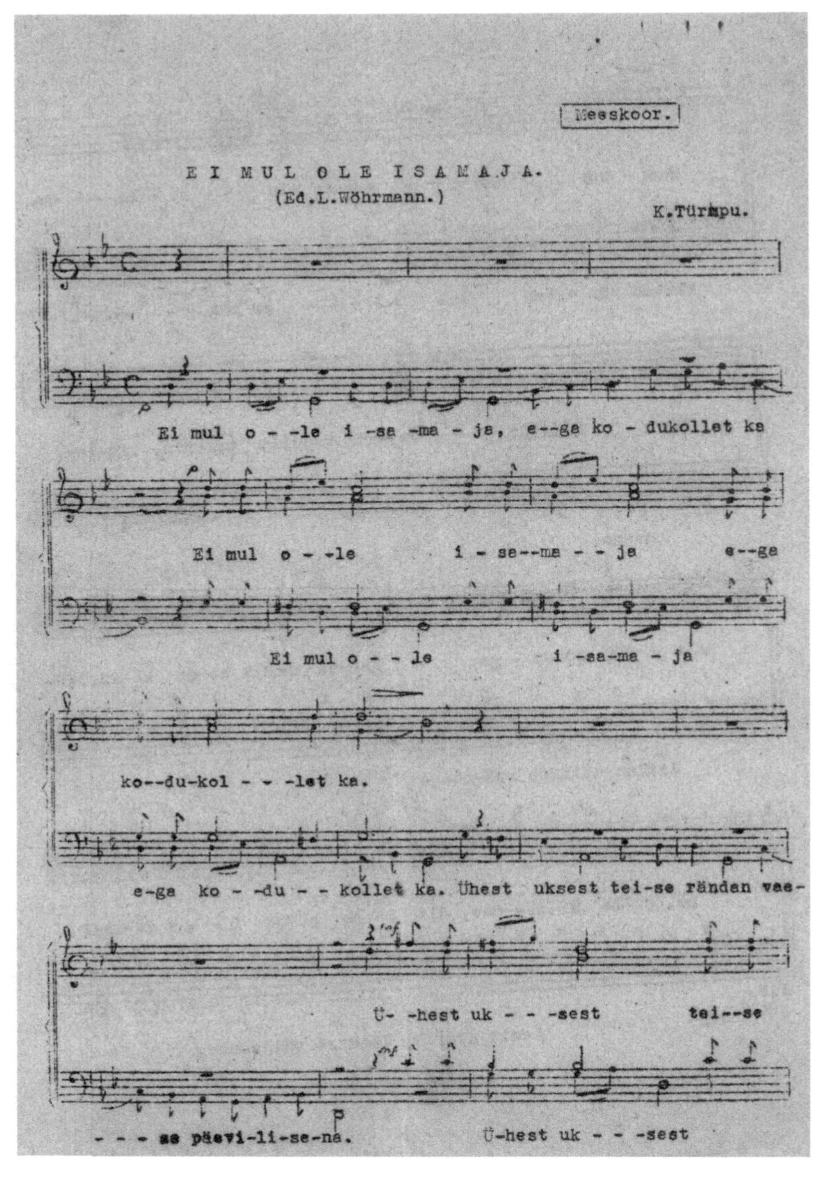

Figure D.16 Türnpu, K. "Ei Mul Ole Isamaja" (ed. L. Wöhrmann) for men's choir, orange paper with typed words. Both sides of the paper printed. "Eesti Kooride Keskuse väljaanne" (Estonian choral center issue).

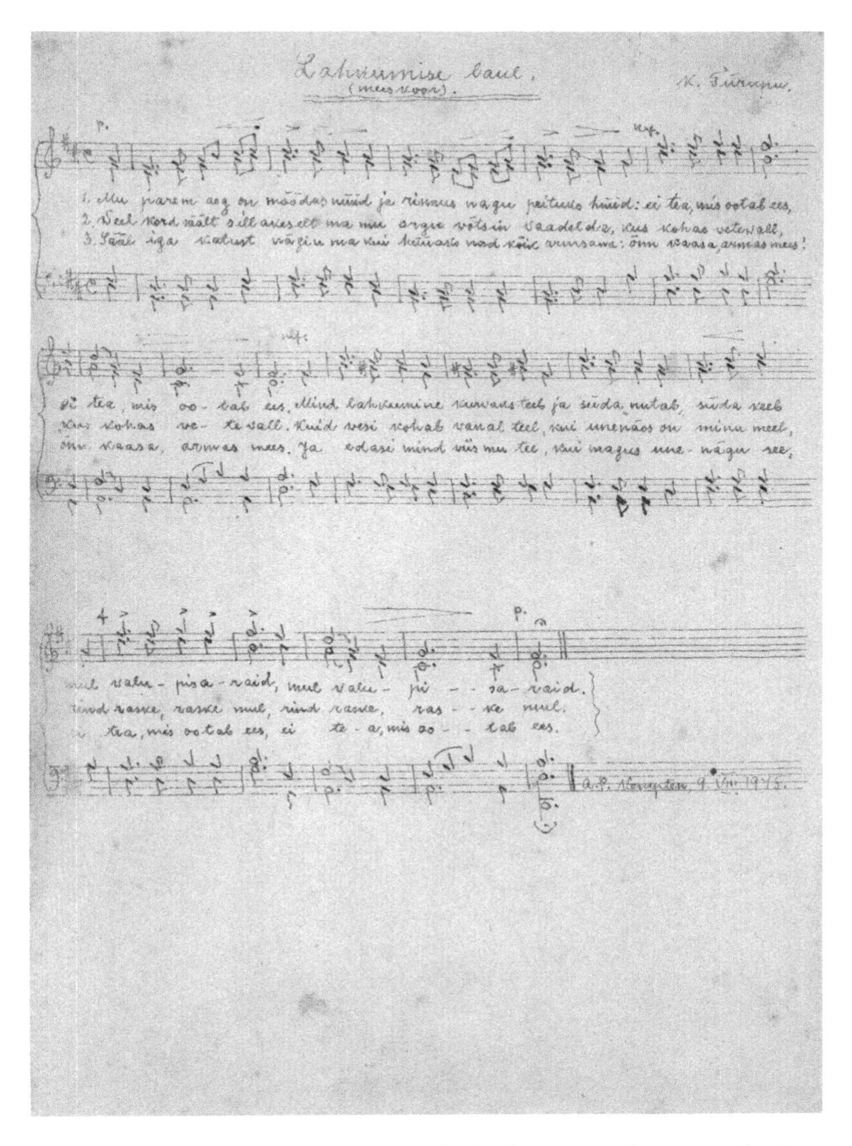

Figure D.17 Türnpu, K. "Lahkumise laul" for men's choir. Handwritten in blue ink on tan paper in A.P. Kempten, July 9, 1945 by L. Mankin, on the back side of another handwritten "Hakkame, mehed minema."

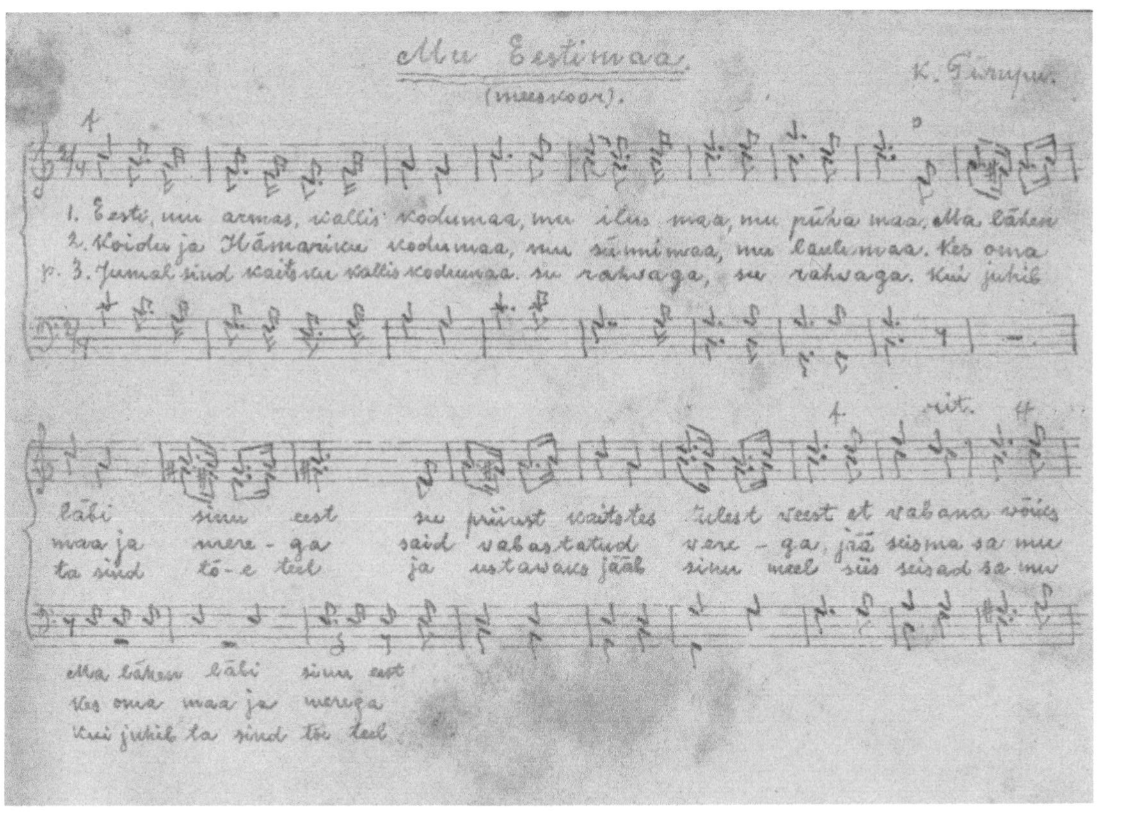

Figure D.18 Türnpu, K. “Mu Eestimaa” for men’s choir. Handwritten in blue ink on small (5 by 8 ½ inch) tan paper, last 2 bars on back side followed by “Tervitus.”

Figure D.19 Vettik, T. "Kaera-Jaan," for mixed choir, handwritten in black ink (probably mimeographed) on tan paper. Follows onto the back side after final stave of "Merella on sinine." Geislingen 1946. "Eesti kooride keskuse väljaanne" (Estonian choir group issue).

Figure D.20 Vettik, T. "Merella on sinine." For mixed choir, handwritten in black ink (probably mimeographed) on tan paper. Follows onto the back side and then "Kaera-Jaan" after that. Geislingen 1946. "Eesti kooride keskuse väljaanne" (Estonian choir group issue).

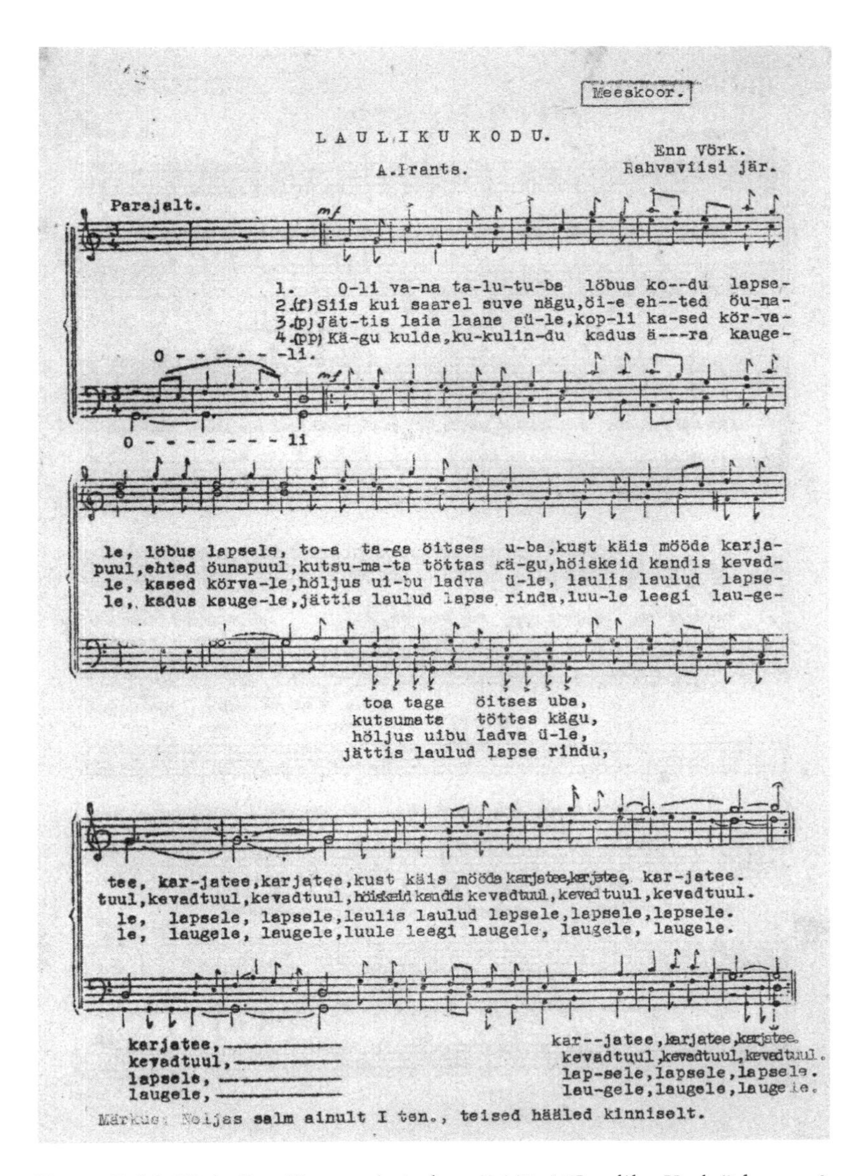

Figure D.21 Võrk, Enn/Prants, A. (rahvaviisi jär.) "Lauliku Kodu" for men's choir. Eesti Meeslaulu Selts (Estonian Men's Choir Organization) Geislingen (Steige), black mimeograph on tan paper on the back side of "Nooruse aeg."

Sources

Written works

Aavik, Juhan. *Estonian Music*. Estonian Information Centre, Stockholm, 1961.
Aavik, Juhan. *Üldsegakoori laulud*. (Combined mixed choir songs) Välis-Eesti Förlag, Stockholm, Sweden, 1948. (24 songs collected by Aavik and printed to use at the 1948 Stockholm Song Festival).
Alet, Evald. "Kogunesime ja olime." (We came together and lived). Personal log, 1945. (sent by daughter, Iivi Turner).
Anderson, Benedict. *Imagined Communities: Reflections on the Origin and Spread of Nationalism*. Verso, New York, 1983.
Ansdal, Gary. *How Music Helps in Music Therapy and Everyday Life*. Augsburg Publishing, Ltd., Farnham, 2014.
Anshal, Anat and David Kipper. "The Influence of Group Singing on Trust and Cooperation". *Journal of Music Therapy*, 25(3), 145–155, 1988.
Artinian, Roubina. "Armenian Choirs in Lebanon, 1930–1980: A Bridge between the Past and the Present". In Boudjikanian, A. (ed.) *Armenians of Lebanon: From Past Princesses and Refugees to Present-Day Community*. The Trilingual Proceedings of the Conference Held in Haigazian University, Beirut, 2009, 131–151.
Aun, Karl. *The Political Refugees: A History of Estonians in Canada*. McClelland and Stuart Ltd, Toronto, 1985.
Austraalia Eestlased 1978. (Australian Estonians 1978) compiled by Valdemar Vilder, Sydney, 1978.
Bakis, Eduard. "DP Apathy". In Murphy, H.B.M. (ed.) *Flight and Resettlement*. UNESCO, Lucerne, Switzerland, 1955, 62–86.
Baltic Refugees and Displaced Persons. Foreword by The Duchess of Atholl, Boreas Publishing Co., London, 1947.
Birka, Ieva. "Can Return Migration Revitalize the Baltics? Estonia, Latvia and Lithuania Engage Their Diasporas with Mixed Results" Migration Policy Institute, https://www.migrationpolicy.org/. Accessed May 8, 2019.
Bradley, Deborah. "We Are All Haunted: Cultural Paradox of Trauma". *Philosophy of Music Education Review*, 28(2), 4–23, 2020.

Carpenter, Inta Gale. "Festival as Reconciliation: Latvian Exile Homecoming in 1990". *Journal of Folklore Research*, 33(2), 93–124, 1996.
Cravens, Richard and Thomas Bornemann. "Refugee Camps in Countries of Asylum and the North American Resettlement Process". In Holtzman, Wayne and Thomas Bornemann (eds.) *Mental Health of Immigrants and Refugees*. Hogg Foundation for Mental Health, The University of Texas, Austin, 1990, 47–63.
Danys, Milda. *DP: Lithuanian Immigration to Canada after the Second World War*. Multicultural History Society of Ontario, Toronto, 1986.
DeNora, Tia. *Music Asylums: Wellbeing Through Music in Everyday Life*. Ashgate, Surrey, 2013.
Dissanayake, Ellen. "Ritual and Ritualization: Musical Means of Conveying and Shaping Emotion in Humans and Other animals". In Brown, Steven and Ulrik Volgsten (eds.) *Music and Manipulation: On the Social Uses and Social Control of Music*. Berghahn Books, New York, 2006, 389–410.
DP Baltic Camp at Seedorf: 1946 1947. UNRRA Team 295 Office, printed in Hamburg, Germany, 1947.
Eastes, Victoria Marita Helga. *The Illusion of Peace: The Fate of the Baltic Displaced Persons 1945–1952*. Master's thesis, Texas A&M University, College Station, TX, 2007.
Eesti Lauljate Liidu (Estonian Singers Union). Valik Ühislaule (A Selection of Songs) "Saateks Teisele Trükile" (Guide to the Second Edition), publisher Eesti Abi (Estonian Aid), New York. No date, but prior to 1949.
Eesti Meeslaulu Seltsi. *Meeskoorilaulude Kogu*, Saksamaal, In the IHRCA collection, Rein Neggo, box 3 of 4, 1948.
Eesti Meestelaulu Paevad 1987 Sydney. 40 anniversary album of Eesti Meeskoor Austraalias, 141 Campbell Street, Surry Hills, Australia, 1987.
Eesti Muusika Biograafiline Leksikon. Valgus, Tallinn, 1990.
Eesti Muusika Infokeskus (Estonian Music Information Centre) http://www.emic.ee/estonian-composers. Accessed 2014.
Eesti Organisatsioonide Liit Läänerannikul. *Üldsegakoori Laulud*. Lääneranniku Eesti Päevad, Portland, Oregon, 2011.
"Eesti Pagulaste Laulupidu" (Estonian refugee song festival), unpublished paper, Augsburg, August 10, 1947.
"Eesti Segakoor 'Runo' Tegevusraamat 1945–1948" (Estonian Mixed Choir "Runo" activity book 1945–1948), Gesilingen, 1948.
Eesti Teatri Ja Muusika Muuseum. *Hulkuja Miina: Miina Härma-kirju ja mälestusi*. Eesti Teatri Ja Muusika Muuseum Raamat, Tallinn, Estonia, 2009.
Elliott, Mark. *Pawns of Yalta: Soviet Refugees and America's Role in Their Repatriation*. University of Illinois Press, Urbana, 1982.
EMA 1947–1997. 50 anniversary album of Eesti Meeskoor Austraalias, 141 Campbell Street, Surry Hills, Australia, 1997.
Epner, Elmer. *Estonia: Progress, Achievement, Fate*. Translated by Elga Mikelson, Published in Augsburg DP Camp, 1948.

"Estonian Displaced Persons 'Assembly Center at Geislingen in Germany", Unpublished paper by The Committee of the Estonian Displaced Persons' Assembly Center in Geislingen, June 1949.

"Estonian Displaced Persons 'Assemble Center at Geislingen in Germany", unpublished document typed by The Committee of the Estonian Displaced Persons' Assembly Center at Geislingen, June 1949.

"Estonian Song and Dance Celebrations" Eesti Laulu ja Tantsupeo SA http://laulupidu.ee/english/history/. Accessed 2013.

Estonian State Commission on Examination of the Policies of Repression. *The White Book: Losses Inflicted on the Estonian Nation by Occupation Regimes 1940–1991*. Estonian Encyclopedia Publishers, Republic of Estonia, 2005.

"Estonians Remember Running for Freedom". *Seattle Post Intelligencer*, July 27, 1982.

Estonia's Occupations Revisited Accounts of an Era. (compiled by Heiki Ahonen, edited by Enn Tarvel) The Kister-Risto Estonian Foundation, Tallinn, Estonia, 2004.

The Facts About Refugees. International Refugee Organisation, Palais Des Nations, Geneva, 1948.

Folkestad, Göran. "National Identity and Music". In Macdonald, Raymond, D. Hargreaves, and D. Miell (eds.) *Musical Identities*. Oxford University Press, Oxford, 2002, 151–162.

Gale, E., S. Enright, C. Reagon, C. Lewis, and R. van Deursen. "A Pilot Study of Quality of Life and Lung Function Following Choral Singing in Cancer Survivors and Their Careers" *Ecancermedicalscience*. www.ncbi.nlm.nih.gov/pubmed/22837766. Accessed 2012.

Goodman, R.D., C.K. Vesely, Ba. Leteca, and C.I. Cleveland. "Trauma and Resilience among Refugee and Undocumented Immigrant Women". *Journal of Counseling and Development*, 95(3), 309–321, 2017.

Hallam, Susan and Raymond MacDonald. "The Effects of Music in Community and Educational Settings". In Hallam, Cross and Thaut (eds.) *The Oxford Handbook of Music Psychology*. Oxford University Press, Oxford, 2009, 775–788.

Hess, Juliet. "Moving Beyond Resilience Education: Musical Counter Storytelling", *Music Education Resource*, 2019.

Hinrikus, Rutt (compiler) and Tiina Kirss (ed.) *Estonian Life Stories*. Central European University Press, Budapest, 2009.

Holborn, Louse, W. *The International Refugee Organization: A Specialized Agency of the United Nations, It's History and Work 1946–1952*.Oxford University Press, London, 1956.

Holmes, Ramona. *Estonian Regilaul*. Master's thesis, University of Washington, Seattle, 1982.

Holtzman, Wayne and Thomas Bornemann. *Mental Health of Immigrants and Refugees*. Hogg Foundation for Mental Health, The University of Texas, Austin, 1990.

Ingleby, David. *Forced Migration and Mental Health: Rethinking the Care of Refugees and Displaced Persons*. Springer, New York, 2005.
Ivask, Ivar. *Baltic Elegies*. World Literature Today, Norman, OK, 1990.
Järvesoo, Elmar. *Balti Ülikooli Eesti Seltsi toimetis*. Yale Books, Toronto, 1991.
Judt, Tony. *Postwar: A History of Europe since 1945*. The Penguin Press, New York, 2005.
Jurison, Jaak. *The Last Train from Estonia*. Kurni Press, Newport Beach, CA, 2016.
Juubeli Laulupeo Juht. Eesti NSV Üldlaupeo Peakomision, Eesti Raamat, Tallinn, 1969.
Kalmann, Helmtuh. "An Overview of the Origins and Development of the West Coast Estonian Days", www.portlandesto.org. Accessed 2018.
Kaskla, Edgar. "The Estonian Community in Southern California 1976–2018", www.eestiselts.com/history. Accessed August 2020.
Kool, Ferdinand. *DP Kroonika: Eesti Pagulased Saksamaal, 1944–1951*. Eesti Arhiiv Uhendriikides, Lakewood, NJ, 1999.
Kumer-Haukanõmm, Kaja and Keiu Telve. "Estonians in the World", https://2017.inareng.ee/en/open-to-the-world/estonians-in-the-world. Accessed 2017.
Kuutma, Kirstin. "Cultural Identity, Nationalism and Changes in Singing Traditions", http://www.folklore.ee/folklore/vol2/ident.htm. Accessed October 2020.
Levi, Erik and Florian Scheding (ed.) *Music and Displacement: Diasporas, Mobilities, and Dislocations in Europe and Beyond*. The Scarecrow Press, Lanhm, MD, 2010.
Lie, Suzanne Stiver, Lynda Malik, Ilvi Jõe-Cannon and Rutt Hinrikus. *Carrying Linda's Stones: An Anthology of Estonian Women's Life Stories*. Tallinn University Press, Tallinn, 2007.
Lin, Keh-Ming. "Assessment and Diagnostic Issues in Psychiatric Care of Refugee Patients". In Holtzman, Wayne and Thomas Bornemann (eds.) *Mental Health of Immigrants and Refugees*. Hogg Foundation for Mental Health, The University of Texas, Austin, 1990, 198–206.
Lippus, Urve. "Transformation of an Institution—The First Soviet Estonian Song Festival". *Musik in Diktaturen des 20. Jahrhunderts: Internationals Symposium and der Bergischen Universität Wuppertal vom 28/29.2.2004*. Are Musik Verlags, Frankfurt, Germany, 2006.
Loersch, Chris and Nathan L. Arbuckle. "Unraveling the Mystery of Music: Music as an Evolved Group Process". *Journal of Personality and Social Psychology* Advance online first publication, November:105(5). Doi: 10.1037/a003691, 2013, 777–798
Lowe, Keith. *Savage Continent: Europe in the Aftermath of World War II*. St. Martin's Press, New York, 2012.
MacDonald, Raymond, David Hargreaves and Dorthy Miell. "Musical Identities". In Hallam, Cross and Thaut (eds.) *The Oxford Handbook of Music Psychology*. Oxford University Press, Oxford, 2009, 759–774.

Maddisson, Mai (compiler and narrator). *Estonia's War Children: A Fractured Generation*. Brioga publishing, Melbourne, Australia, 2015.

Maddisson, Mai. *From Here Began the Journey to Far Off Lands: Hats Off to Estonian War Parents*. Brolga Publishing (self-publishing), Melbourne, AU, 2015.

Mägi, Aino Onno. "Youth: Written When I Was 87–88 Years Old", translated and edited by Taimi Ene Moks, unpublished document, 1996.

Mannik, Lynda. *Photography, Memory and Refugee Identity: The Voyage of the SS Walnut, 1948*. UBC Press, Vancouver, 2013.

Manning, Clarence. *The Forgotten Republics*. Philosophical Library, New York, 1952.

Martin, Helle Ajango. *Our Journey Toward Freedom: One Family's Search for Freedom during and After World War II*. Little Miami Publishing Co., Milford, OH, 2009.

Menius, F.R. *Syntagma de origine Livonoram*. Dorpat, 1632, Riga and Leipzig, 1848.

Merits, Helga. *Coming Home Soon: The Refugee Children of Geislingen*. Merits Productions, Tartu, Estonia, 2018.

Moks, Taimi Ene. "Displaced Persons (DP) in Germany" unpublished paper, received, 2014.

Mollica, Richard. "Refugee Trauma: The Impact of Public Policy on Adaptation and Disability". In Holtzman, Wayne and Thomas Bornemann (eds.) *Mental Health of Immigrants and Refugees*. Hogg Foundation for Mental Health, the University of Texas, Austin, 1990, 253–260.

Murphy, H.B.M. *Flight and Resettlement*. UNESCO, Lucerne, Switzerland, 1955.

Murphy, Michael. "Introduction". In White, Harry and Michael Murphy (eds.) *Musical Constructions of Nationalism: Essays on the History and Ideology of European Musical Culture 1880–1945*. Cork University Press, Cork Ireland, 2001, 1–15

Museum of Occupation. "Resistance", www.okupatsioon.ee/en/occupation-period-overview/26-vastupanu. Accessed October 2020.

"Music in the Soviet Estonia". www.okupatsioon.ee/en/overviews-1940-1991/12-muusika. Accessed 2020.

Olsen, Dale. *The Chrysanthemum and the Song: Music, Memory and Identity in the South American Japanese Diaspora*. University of Florida Press, Gainesville, 2004.

Olt, Harry. *Estonian Music*. Perioodika, Tallinn, 1980.

Orav, Carl. *We Were Estonian Soldiers: World War II from a Soldier's Viewpoint*. Menu Kirjastus, Tartu, Estonia, 2011.

Parkhurst, Melissa. *To Win the Indian Heart: Music at Chemawa Indian School*. Oregon State University Press, Corvallis, 2014.

Pennar, Jaan. *The Estonians in America 1627–1975: A Chronology and Fact Book*. Oceania Publications, New York, 1975.

Pettai, Raul. "Estonian violin master Meeme Mälgi (1902–1976)". Eestielu, https://eestielu.com/en/culture/culture/194-eesti-viiulimeister-meeme-maelgi-1902-1976. Accessed May 2012.

Pilli, Toivo. *Dance or Die: The Shaping of Estonian Baptist Identity under Communism*. Paternoster, Milton Keynes, 2008.

Plaks, Arved. "Udo Kasemets" *Viieoru Viisid*. December 2004 and "Anton Kasemets: GEG muusika õpetaja". *Viieoru Viisid*, October 2007.

Puderbaugh, Dave. "How Choral Music Saved a Nation: The 1947 Estonian National Song Festivals of Estonian's Soviet Occupation" *The Choral Journal*, 49(4), 28–43, 2008.

Puderbaugh, David John. *My Fatherland Is My Love: National Identity and Creativity and the Pivotal 1947 Soviet Estonian National Song Festival*. DMA thesis, University of Iowa, Iowa, 2006.

Rebane, George. "Geislingen DP Camp Year, 1945–49", http://rebaneruminations.typepad.com/files/geislingen-dp-camp-years_v130608-2.pdf. Accessed May 11, 2013.

Rebane, George. "Surviving Augsburg Once More-1945". *Rebane's Ruminations*, http://rebaneruminations.typepad.com/rebanes_ruminations/2010/12/surviving-augsburg-once-more-1945.html#more. Accessed 2010.

Rei, August. *Have the Baltic Countries Voluntarily Renounced Their Freedom?* World Association of Estonians, New York, 1944.

Risto, Conte Keivabu. "ESTO 2019 and the Global Estonian Youth", estofestival.com/en/risto-conte-keivabu-esto-2019-and-th-global-estonian-youth/. Accessed July 26, 2019.

Sanal, Ahmet Muhip and Selahattin Gorsev. "Psychological and Physiological Effects of Singing in a Choir". *Psychology of Music* DOI: 10.1177/0305735613477181, published on line 8 April 2013.

Seaford, Richard. "The Politics of the Mystic Chorus". In Billings, Joshua, Felix Budelmann, and Fiona Macintosh *Choruses, Ancient and Modern*. Oxford University Press, Oxford, 2013, 261–280.

Second World Symposium on Choral Music. The Estonian Choral Society, Tallinn, 1990.

Shephard, Ben. *The Long Road Home: The Aftermath of the Second World War*. The Bodley Head, London, 1988.

Šilbajoris, Rimvydas. "Baltic Identity in the Flow of Time". *Baltic Studies Newsletter*, 1(73), XIX, 1995.

Silove, Derrick. "From Trauma to Survival and Adaptation: Towards a Framework for Guiding Mental Health Initiatives in Post-Conflict Societies". In David Ingleby (ed.) *Force Migration and Mental Health: Rethinking the Care of Refugees and Displaced Persons*. Springer, New York, 2005, 29–52.

Siv, Sichan "Coming to America". In Holtzman, Wayne and Thomas Bornemann (eds.) *Mental Health of Immigrants and Refugees*. Hogg Foundation for Mental Health, The University of Texas, Austin, 1990.

Šmidchens, Guntis. *A Baltic Music: The Folklore Movement in Lithuania, Latvia and Estonia,* 1968–1991. PhD dissertation, Indian University, Bloomington, Indiana, 1996.

Šmidchens, Guntis. "Folk Songs and Nationalism in Estonia", Unpublished paper, 1990.

Šmidchens, Guntis. *The Power of Song.* University of Washington Press, Seattle, 2014.

Soovere, Eric. *Käru ja Kaameraga.* Olion, Tallinn, Shown in "Escape" YOUTUBE from Okupatsioonide museum, 1999.

Statistical Report on Occupational Skills of Care Refugees: US-Zone, Germany. Prepared by Employment Division of International Refugee Organization, reported April 15, 1949.

Steenhuisen, Paul. *Sonic Mosaics.* (interview with composer/conductor Udo Kasemets). The University of Alberta Press, Edmonton, AB, 2009.

Stille, Bernhard. *Vom Balitikum ins Schwabenland Oldenberg,* Anton H. Konrad Verlag, Weissenhorn, 1994.

Stokes, Martin. *Ethnicity, Identity and Music: The Musical Construction of Place.* Berg Publishers, Oxford, 1994.

Strachen, Jeremy. *Music, Communication, Place: Udo Kasemets and Experimentation in 1960s Toronto.* University of Toronto dissertation, Toronto, CA, 2015.

Tammaru, Tiit, Kaja Kumer-Haukanõmm, and Kristi Anniste. "The Formation and Development of the Estonian Diaspora". *Journal of Ethnic and Migration Studies,* 6(7), 1157–1174, August 2010.

Toi, Roman. *Swing-Songs in Estonian Folk Songs.* Paper read at seventh Conference on Baltic Studies, Georgetown University, 1980.

Tönismäe, Signe. *Estonian Displaced Persons in Post-War Germany.* MA thesis, West Virginia University, Morgantown, 2015.

Trevarthen, Colwyn. "Communicative Musicality: The Human Impulse to Create and Share Music". In Hargreaves, Miell and Macdonald (eds.) *Musical Imaginations: Multidisciplinary Perspectives on Creativity, Performance, and Perception.* Oxford University Press, Oxford, 2012, 259–284.

Turino, Thomas and James Lea (eds.). *Identity and the Arts in Diaspora Communities.* Harmonie Park Press, Warren, MI, 2004.

United States Displaced Persons Commission. *The Displaced Persons Commission: First Semi-Annual Report to the President and the Congress,* U. S. Government Printing Office, 1949.

Vahter, Artur. *Aleksander Läte.* Eesti Riiklik Kirjastus, Tallinn, 1963.

Valik Ühislaule. *A Selection of Songs.* Eesti Abi, NY, 1940.

Wong, Ketty. *Whose National Music?: Identity, Mestizaje, and Migration in Ecuador.* Temple University Press, Philadelphia, PA, 2012.

Wyman, Mark. *DPs: Europe's Displaced Persons, 1945–1951.* Cornell University Press, Ithaca and London, 1998.

Archives

Estonian Archives in the United States (EAU), Immigration History Research Center Archives, University of Minnesota (IHRCA). Series 1 contains documents and papers regarding camps in US, French and British zones of occupation—mainly about Estonian schools in DP camps, Estonian National Committees, National Groups and other organizations, Estonian Red Cross Committees and UNRRA-IRO [United Nations Relief and Rehabilitation Administration-International Refugee Organization] as well as various documents (correspondence, articles, reports, memoranda, bulletins, newsletters, lists, meeting minutes, regulations, instructions etc.) concerning DP-status and emigration. Series 1 consists of 7 subseries and 26 boxes (1. Camp Augsburg-Hochfeld, boxes D1–D6 2. Camp Geislingen, boxes D7–D8 3. Camps in US Occupation Zone, boxes D9–D16 4. Camps in French Occupation Zone, boxes D17–D18 5. Camps in British Occupation Zone, boxes D19–D25 6. Red Cross and Gold Fund, boxes D25–D26 7. Miscellaneous, box D26), where box D23 contains 2828 cards with biographical information on Estonian prisoners of war in Uklei Camp.

The Estonian Archives in Australia, Sydney Estonian House, 141 Campbell St. Surry Hills, Australia, Maie Barrow archivist.

Box DP elud

3 aastat Geislingin
Fotoalbum 1946–1948
Augsburg Laulupidu kava 1947
Salga päevik, handwritten journal beginning Sept. 2, 1945, entry re: music June 18, 1946.
"Eesti Segakoor 'Runo' tegevusraamat 1945–1948." Geislingen, Nov. 1948.
"Kempten Eesti Segakoori Teise Aastapaewa Kontsert" program.
"Laulud: Eesti Vabariigi 30.Aastapaeva" 1948 kempten program.
"Eesti Vabariigi 29. Aasta paeva Aktus" 1947 Kempten.
"Estonian DP Camp Hanau Estonian Mixed Choirs concert" program 28,9.1947.
"Konsert kaasaegsest heliloomingust" April 17, 1948, Geislingen
"Estonian Song Festival at Kempten" invite, Sept. 20, 1948, Kempten.
"Laulud: leeriõpilaste õnnistamisel" church program, Geislingen, May 16, 1948 and May 25, 1947.
Pildipost. Geislingen DP camp newspaper:
12 August 1947. Augsburg song festival pictures and report.
Map of "Germany: Map of the Occupation Areas."
Im Ausland
3, 1. August 1947 "Estnisches Sängerfest in Augsburg."

#4 20 August 1947 "Kundgebung für Estland."

Kauge Kodu, This journal/newspaper was produced for the Kempten and Altenstadt Estonians as an information bulletin of Eesti Rahvasgruppe. "Published on approval of UNREA." It includes articles about war progress, who is entering and leaving DP camps, announcements of concerts, rehearsals, sports, theater, and culture/politics articles, i.e., an article on "Stalin Kandideere Tallinas" followed by an announcement of a ping-pong tournament.

3, June 30, 1945 "Rahvusliku laulu ja muusika osatähtsus praegusel silmapilgul."

7, July 14, 1945, "Balti Kontserdi Kolmas Päev." (Describes the upcoming program of Latvian, Lithuanian and Estonian choir music. The Estonian mixed choir will sing ...)

#15, August 11, 1945. "Konstantin Türnpu ja Eesti Meeskoorilaulu Areng" (article about an important Estonian composer and men's choir arranger).

#16 August 15, 1945 "Eesti Hümn: Kas algupärane või some-ungari mõjude ristlainete laps?"

22 March 20, 1946, "Haunstetteni Segakoor Altenstadtis."

#26 September 19, 1945, "Laupäeval ja pühapäeval Ernö Kochi maalide näitus." And "Pandi Alus Eesti Kooride Keskusele USA Tsoonis: Koorijuhid olid Geislingenis koos."

#29 September 29, 1945 "Henry Visnapuu 55 Aastane Luuletaja töötab praegu drama 'Kuningas Juhan' kallal" (article about the important Estonian composer's 55th birthday and his songs and works).

#34, 17.Okt.1945 "Laulukoor sai sobivad harjutusruumid"

#39 May 22, 1946 "Elada, Laulda, Laulda ja Surra, Elad Eestile! Geislingeni eesti Meeslaulu Seltsi kontsert altenstadtis 17. Mail." Written by Roman Toi (about the concert by the Geislingen men's choir.)

#40 May 26, 1946 "Eesti Laul" and article about the song festival tradition.

#42 June 1, 1946 "Laulu ja Muusikategelaste kokkutulek Altenstadtis" and "Kaks Sisukat Muusikalist Üritust."

#44 June 8, 1946, "Laagri Segakooril Seljataga Aasta Tööd."

#47 June 18, 1946 "Rahvusgruppide esimehed avaldavad dir. Wishjkule tanu."

#51 July 13, 1946 "Kooride Keskus Kujuneb Muusika Suurorganisatsiooniks."

#52 July 16 "Kolm suurt lapivad kokku aatomi asjus. Nelja-võimu kontroll Jaapanile" war news and radio concert reported in same article.

#53 July 20, 1946 "Estonia Kontsertsaal."

#57 August 2, 1946 article by Roman Toi "Geislingeni Laulpäeva Eelõhtul" and announcement about "Kontsert laulupäeva Kavast."

#61 August 17, 1946 "Kilde Kultuurielu Alalt" note about solist Arno Niitof, baritone concert, Composer Roman Toi new song and H. Visnapuu song.

#69 September 1946" Ilmub H. Visnapuu Luuletuste Valikkogu 'Tuuline Teekord'." "Balti Kontsert" announcement.

#71 September 21, 1946 "R. Toi Siirdub Geislingeni Meeskoori Juhiks."

#81 October 26, 1946 "Ka Muusika on Kodanlik!"
Sõnumid. (Lubeck newspaper)
#2 November 3, 1945. "Üle 30 eesti kontserdi" and "Flensburgi meeskoor kontsertreisil."

Audiovisual documents

Merits, Helge "Coming Home Soon", Merits Productions, 2018.
"Our New Home: Meie Uus Kodu: Estonian Australian Stories" in Powerhouse Museum, Sydney Australia, September 28, 2008.
"Tales from a Suitcase: Interview with Elmar Saarepere" Estonian Australian Archives, 1997.
Tusty, James and Maureen, *The Singing Revolution*. Mountain View Productions, 2006.

Interviews

Kalamae, Raivo, October 1, 2008, Sydney Australia, Estonian Archives.
Kukk, Jaak, July 1995, in Portland (from Woodland Hills, CA), phone 8/27/08.
Liikane, Juhan, LEP Portland 1996 (from San Rafael, CA).
Mägi, Aino, April 1991 and May 3, 1995, Seattle, WA.
Mikelson, Elga, September 6, 2013.
Plaks, Arved, Seattle, 1995, LEP Portland 1996 and letter 7/14/95 and email 8/2008.
Salasoo, Inno (from Roseville, Australia) LEP 1996 Portland.
Shuey, Hilve, Seattle, April 1991.
Siimpoeg, Edgar, October 2, 2008, Estonian Village Thirlmere, Australia.
Toi, Dr. Roman, Toronto, Canada October 7, 1996.
Phone interview, July 29, 2013.
Urv, Elvi, 8/8/96 Portland (from Parkland, WA), phone interview Tacoma, 8/15/20.
Urv, Sulev, 8/8/96 Portland (from Parkland, WA).
Valk, Viktor, October 7, 2008, Northbridge, Australia.
Vesilind, Priit, January 22, 1014, phone conversation from NV.
Virkhaus, Taavo, LEP 8/8/96 Portland and email and phone 8/200.

Index

Note: *Italic* page numbers refer to figures.

Made in the USA
Middletown, DE
01 September 2023

37796049R00106